Toward an Economic Theory of
Income Distribution

M.I.T. Monographs in Economics

Toward an Economic Theory of Income Distribution

Alan S. Blinder

The MIT Press
Cambridge, Massachusetts, and London, England

This book was printed on Decision 94
and bound in Columbia Millbank Vellum MBV-4376
by The Colonial Press Inc.
in the United States of America.

Second printing, first MIT Press paperback edition, 1977

Library of Congress Cataloging in Publication Data

Blinder, Alan S.
  Toward an economic theory of income distribution.

  (M.I.T. monographs in economics, 11)
  Bibliography: p.
  1. Income—Mathematical models. 2. Income—United States—Mathematical models. I. Title. II. Series.
  HB601.B53   339.2'01   74-5417
  ISBN 0-262-02114-5 (hardcover)
  ISBN 0-262-52041-9 (paperback)

To Madeline

Contents

Preface

The research reported here originated as a doctoral dissertation written at the Massachusetts Institute of Technology during the 1970–1971 academic year. It has continued to evolve, in sporadic bursts of activity separated by lengthy periods of inaction, during the past three years at Princeton University.

While an author's evaluation of his own work should be treated with a healthy dose of skepticism, if not utterly disregarded, it seems to me that the intervening three years have not made this work as obsolete as I would have imagined in 1971. In those days it appeared, at least to a graduate student single-mindedly immersed in the study of income distribution, that the profession was on the verge of a burgeoning of interest in inequality, that the economic "pie" had at last grown large enough so that more attention could be paid to its division and less to its size.

The events of the past three years have belied these lofty expectations, especially in so far as theoretical work is concerned. While more research has probably been published in this field during the last three years than in the preceding three, it is hard to argue that the increase has exceeded the growth rate of economic literature in general. And the university that offers a course on income distribution is still the exception rather than the rule. This is unfortunate, since I believe that the field is a fertile one for the application of rigorous economic analysis. And I still think Ricardo was right when he remarked that no problem in economics is so important as the determination of the distribution of income. It is surely no false modesty to state that this book raises many more questions than it answers. My hope is that other economists, finding the questions interesting and the techniques worth pursuing, will join in the development of a coherent theory of income distribution.

My debts are many. Peter Diamond and Robert Solow were my principal advisers while I was working on the dissertation, and their perceptive evaluations of my early work assisted me in formulating many of the ideas expressed here and, most importantly, enabled me to avoid numerous pitfalls. Robert Hall joined my committee when the thesis was nearly finished, and offered astute comments on a complete draft. I also benefited from conversations with Christian von Weizsäcker, Robert Merton, and several others at MIT that year.

Since then many individuals have read bits and pieces of the manuscript as the thesis was laboriously being turned into a book. My former colleague at Princeton, Daniel Hamermesh, must be singled out for having had the perseverance to read and offer valuable comments upon the entire manuscript in its penultimate form. Ray Fair, A. B. Atkinson, and Gregory Chow also offered suggestions which materially improved the content of the final version.

Research assistance was provided, at various times during the 1972–1973 and 1973–1974 academic years by Dennis Warner, Barry Schwartz, Donald Coes, and Edward Meyer. I thank them all. Betty Kaminski did her usual fine job of typing the manuscript.

One ought never to forget his benefactors. As a graduate student, my research was supported by a National Defense Education Act Fellowship to MIT, and for the past two years the National Science Foundation has provided generous financial assistance under Grant GS-36027.

Finally, and most importantly, my sincerest "thank you" is due my wife, Madeline, who has been unfairly subjected to double jeopardy by this monograph—first as a dissertation which stubbornly refused to be banished from our household, and then as a book which preoccupied me far too long. She has had the patience to put up with me as I scratched out the manuscript, and even contributed to its completion by proofreading and correcting my faltering grammar. I am indeed grateful.

For myself, I am content to claim full credit for all remaining errors and omissions.

A. S. B.
Princeton, New Jersey
January 1974

Toward an Economic Theory of
Income Distribution

1
Desiderata for an Economic Theory of Size Distribution

The body of economic analysis rather desperately needs a reliable theory of the distribution of incomes. Whether or not this approach is ultimately deemed to be satisfactory, it should demonstrate that such a theory need not be a patchwork of Pareto distributions, ability vectors, and ad hoc probability mechanisms, but can rely on the basic economic principles that have so often proven their worth elsewhere.

Gary S. Becker

The title of this study is used advisedly. Much of what has been offered in the literature as "economic" models of the size distribution of income and wealth hardly merits the name. That is, while often elegant and ingenious, these models have not been integrated into the mainstream of modern economic theory. This is both inexplicable and unfortunate, since there is a considerable body of economic theory which can be brought to bear on the subject. I hope, within the following chapters, to demonstrate that this is so, and to point the way toward a theory of income distribution which is part of the corpus of neoclassical economic thought. Of course, I take only a few small steps in this direction; hence the use of the word "toward" in the title. The most interesting contributions to the economic theory of size distribution are yet to come.

Most of the work in economics that goes by the name "income distribution theory" has focused on the distribution of income among *factors of production*, rather than the distribution among *individuals*. This orientation dates back at least to Ricardo and Marx and may have been appropriate to the capitalism of the day. While the behavior of distributive shares may still pose interesting intellectual problems in positive economics, its normative significance for inequality as a social problem is nowadays rather limited. But a comparably rigorous theory of size distribution has not been developed. Jan Tinbergen's remark of some years ago [1956, p. 244] seems equally appropriate today: "The fairly satisfactory state of affairs with respect to the statistical description of income distribution contrasts with an unsatisfactory state in the area of economic interpretation."

The remainder of this chapter outlines the requirements for a complete and exact microeconomic theory of the size distribution of income and wealth. I am by no means prepared to meet all of these requirements here. However, by synthesizing some established pieces of economic theory and filling in a few gaps, it is possible to develop a rigorous, though simplified, model of income distribution under capitalism. This is the program for the book. Chapters 2 and 3 provide the microeconomic building blocks, and Chapters 4 to 6 exploit these results to see what economic theory has to say about the size distribution of income in the United States.

1.1 Intragenerational and Intergenerational Models of Size Distribution

There are two separate aspects of distribution theory which are best distinguished at the outset. An *intragenerational* model is designed to answer the question, Why is the income distribution what it is today? Its principal components are models of the savings, consumption, investment, training, and labor supply behavior of individual consumer units. It takes as given the wealth, technology, and abilities inherited from previous generations. An *intergenerational* model is designed to answer the question, What factors determine the evolution of the income distribution over time? It focuses on decisions to bequeath wealth, both human (through education) and nonhuman (through inheritance), to one's heirs. The inheritance of genetic ability, though not subject to human choice (yet!), also plays a role here.

The two models complement each other in a straightforward way: each provides the "initial conditions" for the other. For example, a fully developed intragenerational model would have to generate the distribution of bequests since the latter is an integral part of savings behavior and wealth accumulation. Appending to this some model— and none has been suggested to date—of parental decisions to educate their offspring would close the loop between the income distribution in one generation and the income distribution among its successors.

This study is confined to the intragenerational model though it will have something to say about bequest behavior.[1] To the extent that they have contained any behavioral aspects at all, most previous efforts have also been confined to intragenerational aspects. The reader unfamiliar with the size distribution literature may be startled to learn that there are income distribution models devoid of behavioral content. But in fact, such models—generally based on some sort of stochastic process—are among the best known distribution theories.

1.2 Models of the Size Distribution: A Survey[2]

1.2.1 Stochastic Process Models

The fact that income distributions appear quite stable over time has suggested to several authors that the distribution might be the steady-state solution of some stochastic process. Robert Gibrat [1957] seems to have originated this line of thought when he noted that the *product* of a large number of independent random variables tends toward the lognormal distribution,[3] which has the positive skewness displayed by the data, rather than toward the symmetric normal distribution, which is the limit of the sum of additive errors. This multiplicative central limit theorem leads naturally to the following simple Markov model, which Gibrat dubbed "the law of proportional effect." Let income in period t be denoted by Y_t. Assume that Y_t is generated by a first-order Markov process, so that it depends only on Y_{t-1} and stochastic influences. Specifically,

$$Y_t = R_{t-1} Y_{t-1},$$

where $\{R_t\}$ is a sequence of serially independent random variables which are independent of Y_t. If Y_0 is income in the initial period, it follows immediately that

$$Y_t = Y_0 \cdot R_0 \cdot R_1 \cdot R_2 \cdot \ldots \cdot R_{t-1}.$$

The multiplicative central limit theorem implies that as t gets large, the distribution of Y_t tends toward the lognormal.

1. For the beginnings of a crude intergenerational model, the reader is referred to Blinder [1973b]. Other relevant references are Stiglitz [1969], Atkinson [1971], Ishikawa [forthcoming], and Pryor [1969].
2. Other surveys of the theoretical literature have been offered by Bjerke [1961], Lydall [1968], and Mincer [1970].
3. If $y = \log x$, and y is normal, then x is said to have the lognormal distribution.

Other than the serial independence of the R_t, one troubling feature of this model is its implication that the variance of $\log(Y_t)$ is steadily increasing, a prediction which is belied by the data. Michal Kalecki [1945] has modified the simple Gibrat model by introducing a negative correlation between Y_t and R_t which is just sufficient to prevent the log variance of Y_t from growing. Economically, this means that the probability that income will rise by a given percentage is lower for the rich than for the poor. It is far from obvious that this is true. In a way, Kalecki's contribution is a microcosm of the entire stochastic process approach: it is highly ingenious, but equally *ad hoc*.

Other than the lognormal, the analytical distribution which is used most frequently to fit the data is the Pareto distribution

$$N(Y) = AY^{-\alpha},$$

where $N(Y)$ is the fraction of the population having income greater than Y and A and α are constants. Over fifty years elapsed between Pareto's remarkable empirical discovery that the upper tails of almost all income distributions followed this law and D.G.Champernowne's [1953] elegant demonstration that, under suitable assumptions, the stationary income distribution must approximate the Pareto irrespective of the initial distribution. Like Gibrat, Champernowne views the income determination process as a Markov process, so that one's income for this period depends only on one's income for the last period and random influences. But, unlike Gibrat, he subdivides income into a finite number of classes and defines transitional probabilities p_{ij} as the probability of being in class j at time $t+1$, given that one was in class i at time t. The crucial assumptions of Champernowne's analysis concern the definition of the income classes and the specification of the transitional probabilities. The income intervals defining each class are assumed to form a geometric progression rather than the conventional arithmetic progression. That is, the limits of class k are higher than the limits of class $k-1$ by a certain *percentage* rather than by a certain absolute amount of income. Most crucial to his result is the assumption that the transitional probabilities p_{ij} depend only on the differences $j-i$. Under these and certain other assumptions,[4] Champernowne proves that the distribution eventually behaves like the Pareto law.

---

4. Among the other assumptions are (1) incomes cannot move up more than one interval, nor down more than n intervals, in any one year; (2) there is a lowest interval, beneath which no income can fall; (3) the average number of intervals shifted in a year is negative in every income bracket.

Champernowne's result can be generalized in several directions. For example, a Pareto distribution can be derived in a model where people fall into groups (say, by age or occupation), and where stochastic movements from one group to another are allowed. But, as he recognizes, several assumptions cannot be dispensed with. Of course, no Markov process yields a stationary distribution unless the matrix of transitional probabilities is constant forever. This is obvious enough; but it is hard to imagine a society whose institutional framework is so static as this. Secondly, his assumption that the probabilities of advancing or declining are independent of the size of income is crucial. Many people who believe in "inherited privilege" or the "cycle of poverty" will not find this a congenial notion. Finally, J. Aitchison and J. A. C. Brown [1954] have shown that a minor alteration in one of his assumptions—specifically making the p_{ij} depend on the *ratio j/i* rather than the *difference $j - i$*—makes the model generate the lognormal distribution rather than the Pareto. It is difficult to argue that either assumption is more plausible than the other.

Another difficulty with Champernowne's model, as with Gibrat's, is that stochastic processes like these may take a very long time to approach their stationary states. If initial conditions are to be unimportant, this requires that an "income" be passed on at death from one person to the next, so that we are not dealing with the incomes of finite-lived individuals but rather with the incomes of infinite families. R. S. G. Rutherford [1955] has explicitly incorporated birth-and-death considerations into a Markov model. Under the assumptions that (1) the supply of new entrants grows at a constant rate, (2) these people enter the labor force with a lognormal distribution of income, and (3) the number of survivors in each cohort declines exponentially with age, he deduces that incomes will eventually approximate the Gram-Charlier Type A distribution, which, he claims, fits the data better than the lognormal. Aside from being a step in the direction of greater realism, the advantage of Rutherford's model is that it offers an alternative to Kalecki's method for insuring that the log variance of income does not grow over time. In Rutherford's model, unlike Kalecki's, the shocks are independent of income, so that the variance of $\log(Y_t)$ grows over time *within each age cohort*; but the cohort with the largest variance dies each year, and a new cohort with a small variance is born. Thus Rutherford is able to show that the overall variance of $\log(Y_t)$ is constant over time.

Benoit Mandelbrot [1961], perhaps the chief proponent of the Pareto distribution, has shown that the income distribution must eventually approximate the Pareto in a Markov model very similar to Champernowne's, but one which does not require the strict law of proportionate effect (that is, that the random shocks be additive in the logs). He has also stressed several desirable statistical properties of what he calls "weak Pareto laws," that is, frequency distributions that are asymptotic to the Pareto. First of all, consider the overall distribution of income as a weighted average of many components, for example, incomes in different occupations or incomes from different sources. Suppose further that the distributions of these components all follow some probability law. If the overall income distribution also follows this probability law, Mandelbrot calls it a "stable distribution." It turns out that the only stable distributions are the normal—which is known not to fit income distribution data—and the family of weak Pareto laws [Mandelbrot, 1960]. The second convenient property of the Pareto family is as follows. If one considers the limit distribution of the sum of a large number of independent and identically distributed random variables, one arrives at the normal distribution only by further assuming that the *largest* of the components is negligible in size. If, as Mandelbrot believes is more common in economic applications, the largest component is not negligible, then the limit distribution follows a weak Pareto law [Mandelbrot, 1961].

A final stochastic model that generates the Pareto distribution was offered by H. O. A. Wold and P. Whittle [1957]. Their model is meant to apply to stocks of wealth, which grow at a compound interest rate during the lifetime of a wealth-holder and then are divided among the heirs at death. They assume that deaths occur randomly with a known mortality rate per unit time. Applying this model only to wealth above a certain minimum,[5] they derive the Pareto law and express the exponent α as a function of the number of heirs per person, the growth rate of wealth, and the mortality rate.

The probabilistic school of thought culminates in a brilliant but almost unknown paper by J. D. Sargan [1957]. Sargan's model can be thought of as a continuous Markov process, where the ways in which transitions occur are explicitly spelled out. The great virtue of the model is its generality: it can accommodate almost any probability distributions for (1) setting up of new households and dissolving of old ones, (2) gifts from one household to another, (3) savings and capital gains, (4) inheritances. This list incorporates, I believe, most

5. This is necessary because the Pareto distribution only applies above some positive minimum wealth.

of the reasons economists would give for changes in household wealth. Unfortunately, the very generality of the model makes it unwieldy (not to mention unintelligible), and Sargan has to settle for analysis of a special case. In this instance, the stochastic process eventually leads to a distribution which is approximately lognormal.

What do all these stochastic models contribute to an economist's understanding of income distribution? In my opinion, not very much. Assuming a stochastic mechanism, no matter how complex, to be the sole determinant of income inequality is to give up before one starts. It is antithetical to the mainstream of economic theory which seeks to explain complex phenomena as the end result of deliberate choices by decision-makers. Borrowing terms from the econometric literature, one may think of the deterministic part of any model as "what we (think we) know" and the stochastic disturbance as the measure of our ignorance. The probabilistic approach to distribution theory appears to allocate the entire variance in income to the latter. One would hope that economics could do better than that.

An important first step in this direction was taken in a paper by Milton Friedman [1953]. I classify Friedman's model with the stochastic theories since the income distribution that it generates is a drawing from a random process. But, unlike the other stochastic models, individual choices by persons differing in risk aversion help determine the shape of the distribution. Roughly speaking, Friedman views every person as having a certain income and an opportunity to participate in a lottery if he so desires. Each person consults his utility function, and the less risk averse enter the lottery while the more risk averse do not. The resulting income distribution is an amalgam of three distributions, each one of which could be symmetrical: (1) nonparticipants; (2) lottery losers, whose distribution has a slightly lower mean; and (3) lottery winners, whose distribution has a much higher mean. If the lottery has only a few winners of very large prizes, the resulting overall distribution is positively skewed with an elongated upper tail.

Certainly the papers by Friedman, Sargan, and Wold-Whittle make it clear that, if the stochastic process theories are to play any role in a model of size distribution, they are most appropriately used to analyze the accumulation of risky capital. Here random elements are likely to predominate, although there are still economic considerations in choosing an optimal portfolio. It may well be no accident that the upper tails of almost all income distributions, where returns to capital dominate and earnings play a minor role, exhibit a striking resemblance to the Pareto distribution. Models like those of Champernowne, Mandelbrot, and Wold-Whittle may well hold the key to this phenomenon.

The model of income distribution to be presented in the following chapters is exact and nonstochastic. A more complete and realistic model would allow for random elements, perhaps along the lines suggested by these models.

1.2.2 Ability-Earnings Models

Most of income consists of earnings, and stochastic models appear to have little to say about this type of income. Of course, this does not mean that the laws of probability theory are not useful in this context. If earnings depend on ability (however measured), and the distribution of ability follows some known frequency distribution, it may be possible to deduce the functional form of the income distribution from the distribution of abilities. A second school of thought, which seeks to exploit this simple idea, has arisen.

Theorizing of this sort appears to have been started by Otto Ammon's [1899] early observation that incomes follow a skewed distribution while abilities are apparently normally distributed.[6] Ammon attributed this discrepancy to quirks in the income tax data which he used and to altruism, which prevented those with unusually low ability from having such low incomes.

This explanation was deemed unsatisfactory by many economists. Most notably, A. C. Pigou, in his monumental *The Economics of Welfare* [1924], pointed out two reasons why the income distribution might be skewed despite the normal distribution of abilities. First, part of income is attributable to inherited wealth, including the opportunities for increasing one's earnings that large inheritances typically bring. And it was well known, even then, that inheritances follow a highly skewed distribution. Secondly, Pigou suggested that the overall distribution of earnings might be skewed because it is an amalgam of the distributions within "noncompeting" subgroups of the population. His example was "brain-workers" versus "hand-workers," and he suggested that the across-group competition was minimal. Pigou speculated that the distributions among brain-workers and hand-workers might each be normal, and yet the overall distribution could be skewed. Some years later, Hans Staehle [1943] offered some evidence from U.S. and German data to support

6. A convenient summary of the early literature, beginning wth Ammon, can be found in Staehle [1943], Part I.

Pigou's conjecture, and Herman Miller's [1955a, 1955b] thorough examinations of U.S. Census data have established that income distributions for relatively homogeneous subgroups of the population tend to be much more symmetric than the overall distribution.

Staehle offered yet another explanation of skewness, which ought to have been obvious to economists long before. Ability is, presumably, a proximate determinant of the *wage rate* (potential earnings) rather than of earnings. If individual supplies of work effort respond positively to higher wages, hours of work and wage rates are positively correlated, so that their product—earnings—is positively skewed even if both wages and hours are symmetric. Alternatively, if the variation in hours worked is mostly due to involuntary unemployment and if employers lay off their least skilled workers more freely than their skilled workers, positive correlation between wages and hours again arises.

The notion that products of normally distributed variates are generally positively skewed has stimulated several models of earnings distributions, beginning with C. H. Boissevain [1939]. He simply observed that if earnings depend in a multiplicative way on various factors ("skills"), then the distribution of earnings is skewed even if all the factors are uncorrelated and normally distributed. This result may be generalized and somewhat sharpened by noting that the multiplicative central limit theorem, which Gibrat applied to random shocks over time, can also be applied cross sectionally. That is, the lognormal distribution tends to result if earnings are a product of a large number of independent factors, even if those factors are not normally distributed.

A. D. Roy has applied these ideas to income distribution in a series of papers. In his simplest model [Roy, 1950a], he asserts that earnings are proportional to output produced, and that output is the product of speed, accuracy, and hours of work. Assuming each of these three factors to be normally distributed, though correlated, he appeals to some results of J. B. S. Haldane [1942] to show that the earnings distribution is approximately lognormal if the coefficients of variation of the three factors are about equal. Roy's case is strengthened once it is observed that the coefficients of variation of speed, accuracy, and hours worked are not in fact equal. For then his model places more people in the upper tail of the distribution than the lognormal would predict, and Harold Lydall [1968] has documented the fact that actual income distributions have fatter tails than the lognormal. In a later paper, Roy [1951] takes an important first step toward making his model less mechanistic by allowing each individual to choose the job in which he earns the highest income. He argues that the resulting income distribution still resembles the lognormal.[7]

A somewhat different ability-earnings model, using precisely that same mathematical result, was offered by Thomas Mayer [1960] some ten years after Roy. He argues for the empirical validity of the notion that earnings depend on the product of the probability of completing a task successfully (which he calls "ability") and the scale of the activity (which he calls "responsibility"). As I have just noted, if ability and responsibility are normally and independently distributed with equal coefficients of variation, this leads precisely to a lognormal earnings distribution. Of course, Mayer believes that these two determinants of earnings are positively correlated; but this still yields an "almost lognormal" distribution. Significantly, Mayer's paper may be the first example of an economist questioning the underlying assumption that abilities are normally distributed. Lydall [1968] has shown that this belief is based on perilously little evidence.

All of the ability-earnings models cited so far seek to explain how a skewed income distribution might arise from a normal distribution of abilities. A closely related set of models employs somewhat different, and often *ad hoc*, assumptions about individual talents. E. C. Rhodes [1944] suggested the following model to explain the Pareto distribution. Suppose people fall into a finite number of homogeneous classes defined by the number of talents they possess. Suppose further that the number of people with k talents declines with k in a geometric progression, and that the mean income rises with k in a different geometric progression. Finally, suppose that the coefficients of variation are equal in each group, though the within-group distributions are not necessarily normal. Rhodes shows that these hypotheses imply a weak Pareto distribution, although he realizes that his assumptions about the wage structure and the distribution of talents come close to assuming the conclusion.

Lydall [1959] has constructed a similar model, though with a much stronger economic motivation, which he means to apply to the upper tail of the earnings distribution. He argues that in hierarchical organizations a person's earnings depend largely on the number of people he supervises. Let there be k distinct grades in the bureaucracy in question, with one person in the highest grade (the

---

7. A slight change in Roy's assumptions for this model yields a Pareto distribution instead. See below.

company president), $n > 1$ in the second, n^2 in the third, and so on. Under this assumption, the number of workers in grade i and higher is

$$Q_i = 1 + n + n^2 + \cdots + n^{k-i} = \frac{n^{k-i+1} - 1}{n-1},$$

so that the *fraction* of workers in grade i or higher is

$$N_i \equiv \frac{Q_i}{Q_1} = \frac{n^{k-i+1} - 1}{n^k - 1} \approx n^{1-i} \qquad\qquad \text{for large } n,k.$$

Lydall's second crucial assumption is that the earnings of a grade i worker are a fixed fraction p, which is independent of i, of the total earnings of the n grade $i-1$ men he supervises. Thus, if Y_i denotes earnings at level i in the hierarchy, we have

$$Y_{i+1} = pnY_i$$

from which it follows that

$$Y_i = (pn)^{i-1} Y_1.$$

Thus, he provides some economic justification for Rhodes' assumptions that skill groups form a descending geometric progression while wage levels form an ascending geometric progression. The two relations can be solved simultaneously to yield

$$\log N_i = \text{constant} - \alpha \log Y_i,$$

where $\alpha = \log n / \log pn > 1$, which is Pareto's Law.

What Lydall has produced here, of course, is a model that generates a Pareto distribution *within* a single bureaucratic organization. It is a model of the income distribution of the employees of General Motors Corporation, or of the federal government. Only if the key parameters, p and n, are invariant across organizations does the overall income distribution follow the Pareto law. Finally, not all (perhaps not even most) of the workers in the upper tail of the earnings distribution are high-ranking members of hierarchical organizations; think, for example, of doctors and lawyers.

Two other models do not fall quite neatly into the category of ability-earnings models, but are closely related. Mandelbrot [1962] offers an income maximization model similar to Roy's last model but which leads to a weak Pareto law. He assumes that individual i is faced with potential wages in each job j which are a *linear* function of his personal attributes:

$$Y_{ij} = c_j + \sum_k \gamma_{jk} A_{ki},$$

where A_{ki} is the amount of attribute k possessed by individual i, and γ_{jk} is the marginal valuation of attribute k in job j. Each attribute is assumed to have a distribution across individuals which is asymptotic to a Pareto function with the same α, and every individual selects the job that maximizes his income. Under these assumptions, Mandelbrot proves that the resulting income distribution follows a weak Pareto law, though not with the same α as the attributes.

Jan Tinbergen, in a series of papers [1951, 1956, 1957, 1971] has set forth an alternative job selection model, which has a much stronger basis in standard economic theory. The goal of his model is to go behind the almost tautological notion that an individual must be compensated for the disutility attached to his job, and actually analyze the nature of this disutility. Tinbergen defines a "job" by a vector of attributes, $S = (s_1, \ldots, s_n)$, where n may be a very large number. Similarly, each individual can be identified by the vector of attributes he possesses, $\Sigma = (\sigma_1, \ldots, \sigma_n)$. For example, if the third attribute were education, s_3 would be the educational requirement for the job and σ_3 would be the educational attainment of the worker. Tinbergen believes that the disutility of any job is a function of the "tension" between S annd Σ. That is, since a person may feel harried and insecure in a position that is too demanding for him, he must be paid some extra compensation to undertake it. Similarly, since working in a job beneath his capabilities may be demeaning and boring, a monetary incentive must be offered to attract "overqualified" workers.

In selecting a job, each worker faces two sets of "givens." First, he knows his own vector of characteristics Σ; and, second, he is confronted by a given wage structure $w = w(S)$, which describes how rates of pay vary with job characteristics. Note that, unlike the models of Roy and Mandelbrot, Tinbergen makes no particular assumption about the functional form of $w(S)$; instead, this function is to be determined by the model. Also, whereas Roy and Mandelbrot posit income maximization to be the goal of each worker, Tinbergen assumes utility maximization, a more satisfying hypothesis. The arguments of the utility function are income and "tension," which is taken to be a quadratic function of the discrepancies $s_i - \sigma_i$, so that the worker does not in general choose the job that maximizes his income.

Given a wage structure, self-selection by workers yields a distribution of income.[8] How, then, is the equilibrium wage structure determined? By standard supply and demand analysis. Each consumer has a supply of labor functional contingent on his attributes.[9] Aggregating these over all individuals yields an aggregate labor supply functional $L[S;w(S)]$. Similarly, for any wage structure, profit-maximizing firms have a demand for labor; and summing over all firms yields the market labor demand functional $D[S;w(S)]$. Short-run wage determination is simple; the wage structure must adjust so that L equals D at each point S: $L[S;w(S)] = D[S;w(S)]$.[10]

Except in trivially simple cases, this model is far too complex to solve for the functional form of the income distribution; but several interesting properties of the solution can be deduced. For one thing, Tinbergen shows that if education serves to bring the distribution of Σ's closer to the distribution of S's, it equalizes the income distribution. For another, the model makes it clear that an equal income distribution does *not* require that every person have the same Σ vector, but only that the frequency distributions of Σ and S be identical[11] [Tinbergen, 1957].

Taken as a group, these models have much more to offer the economist seeking an understanding of the income distribution mechanism than the stochastic models. For one thing, there is the suggestion that if wages are a *multiplicative* function of various worker characteristics, then the distribution of wage rates is positively skewed even if characteristics are distributed symmetrically and

8. In reality, of course, employees do not have complete freedom to choose any job. Employers typically set some minimum requirements and hire only those workers who meet them.

9. To facilitate the exposition, jobs are assumed to form a continuum. That is, each s_i is assumed to be a continuous variable so that a demand for attributes (possibly zero) exists at every S. This, of course, is not necessary in Tinbergen's theory. Some of the attributes could be discrete characteristics like sex.

10. Even in this simple situation, the questions of existence and uniqueness are far from trivial. The analytical difficulties are essentially those of extending the general equilibrium model to a continuum of commodities. On this see Bewley [1972]. Of course, if S is discrete, the well-known theorems on competitive equilibrium apply immediately.

11. This assumes, following Tinbergen, that every person has the same utility function. These observations certainly suggest that deliberate choices by workers and firms tend to make the distributions of Σ's and S's more alike over time. If perfect equality is not to be the ultimate result, control of workers over Σ and firms over S must be incomplete.

independently. Though not motivated by these models, most recent empirical work on microeconomic wage equations have employed this functional form.[12] Secondly, there is the realization that *earnings* are not the same thing as *wage rates* and therefore need not follow the same probability distribution. Indeed, since hours of work depend on wage rates, the distribution of earnings deviates from the distribution of wages in a systematic and predictable way. Finally, the job selection models of Mandelbrot and Tinbergen point out in a very direct way how rational choice by individual decision-makers helps determine the shape of the distribution.

While all these are definite assets, the liabilities of this school of thought should be obvious. Above all, these models are mostly simplistic in their assumptions. This stems from the desire to deduce a closed analytical form for the income distribution, a goal that this study eschews. Secondly, with the exception of the job selection models, they are completely mechanistic. In this respect, the present study is a marked improvement, though in other respects it may be deemed a step backwards (see below).

1.2.3 The Human-Capital Approach

A potentially more satisfying theory of labor incomes than the ones considered so far has its roots in the work of Jacob Mincer [1958] and Gary Becker [1962, 1964] on the human-capital model. In its simplest form, the human-capital approach consists of a series of definitions and the hypothesis of lifetime income maximization. First, there is an identity relating *potential* earnings X_t at age t, to the potential earnings X_{0t} of an untrained individual and the returns on past human investments:

$$X_t = X_{0t} + r_t H_t,$$

where H_t is the amount of human capital and r_t is the average rate of return. Actual earnings E_t are derived from potential earnings by deducting the current investment in human capital formation (foregone earnings) I_t:

$$E_t = X_t - I_t.$$

And, finally, the stock of human capital is derived in the obvious way

12. See, for example, Blinder [1973a], Hall [1973], Hurd [1971], Boskin [1972], Oaxaca [1973].

from past investments:

$$H_t = \sum_{i=0}^{t} I_{t-i},$$

where this formula can be modified to allow human capital to depreciate if desired.

It is assumed that each individual selects the lifetime pattern of I_t which maximizes his lifetime discounted earnings. The model can also be extended to account for post-schooling investments (on-the-job training). In versions designed for empirical application, the unobservable X_{0t} term is generally neglected; that is, it is assumed to be small relative to the returns on human investment, so that the distribution of X_t can be deduced from the distributions of r_t and H_t, and the correlation between them.[13]

In this model, at last, "economic man" occupies center stage as an individual intent on maximizing something. In so far as each person's demand for human capital is contingent upon his ability, the human-capital model can subsume—at least formally—most of the ability-earnings models. But, through the supply side, it is also capable of accounting for capital market imperfections and the interaction of inherited wealth with access to education. While the model cannot predict a precise functional form for the income distribution—a task far too tall for any realistic theory—it does predict positive skewness and certain relationships among the distributions of ability, training, and earnings. Further, unlike almost all of the models considered so far, it lends itself readily to empirical implementation[14] and theoretical generalization.[15]

While the application of human-capital theory to the distribution of earnings must be considered a milestone in the evolution of size distribution theory, there remain some weaknesses in the basic model which undermine its usefulness as a foundation for income distribution theory. For one thing, the entire approach is based on the nonoperational notion of a "unit of human capital." This is something that has been neither seen nor touched and which some human-capital theorists often seem to tautologically define as "that

13. This brief exposition of human-capital theory follows most closely Becker [1967].
14. See, for example, Becker and Chiswick [1966], Chiswick and Mincer [1972], or Malkiel and Malkiel [1973]. There are many others.
15. Ben-Porath [1967, 1971].

which raises earning power by $r\%$." If a unit of human capital is a measurable quantity—years of education for example—why not call it that? If not, then what is it? In their verbal discussions, as opposed to their simple formal models, human-capital theorists seem to use a much broader notion of human capital, including (at the very least) formal education, on-the-job training, experience, health, and locational decisions. Indeed, Tinbergen's vector of personal attributes Σ may come closer to what they have in mind than any single measure of human capital denominated in dollars. And this vector cannot be reduced to a scalar in any theoretically valid way.[16]

Equally serious is the strange objective function attributed to *homo economicus* by the human-capital school—the maximization of discounted lifetime earnings. Taken literally, this would imply that leisure has no value, a questionable empirical proposition. Put differently, human-capital analysis rigorously applies only to *potential* earnings, but is glibly utilized as a model of *actual* earnings, with little attention paid to labor-supply decisions. While simplification of reality is always a legitimate device for theorists, one wonders whether the human-capital school—like the other two schools of thought considered above—has not assumed away too much in an effort to deduce strong conclusions.

The model to be presented in this book can best be viewed as complementary to the human-capital approach rather than as a substitute for it. It is strong where the human-capital model is weak. In particular, it is derived from explicit utility maximization by households, and labor-leisure choices play an important role. Therefore, it treats separately the wage rate and hours of work, rather than dealing with their product, earnings. Finally, it integrates labor incomes and property incomes into a single model of the size distributions of both income and wealth. But, at this stage at least, it is painfully weak where the human-capital model is strong: it fails to consider educational choices and the distribution of wage rates. It is hoped that a synthesis of this model with the human-capital model will result in a size distribution model which is decidedly superior to either. My work on this more difficult problem is in far too preliminary a state to report here, though I offer some suggestive remarks in Section 1.4.

16. In some ways the problem of defining "human capital" is similar to the aggregation problems that arise almost everywhere in macroeconomics, for example, in defining the aggregate capital stock. The crucial difference, in my opinion, is that, unlike nonhuman capital, human capital is not even a well-defined concept at the micro level.

1.3 A Unified Framework for Distribution Theory

A proper theory of income distribution should begin with a model of the income—from both property and labor—of a given household at a given point of time. I define the "economic vintage" of an individual as his actual birth date plus the length of his childhood (say, eighteen years). This vintage will be assumed to be the date at which he (1) enters the labor force; (2) leaves his parents' home to set up a new household; (3) comes into any inheritance he may receive; and (4) becomes a *homo economicus*, that is, a rational calculating machine that seeks to maximize utility. Before this date, I assume his parents make all important economic decisions for him.

A household will be identified by its head, that is, its vintage will be considered to be the vintage of its head. The entire analysis will be carried out in terms of the preferences of the household, rather than the preferences of a single individual. As Paul Samuelson [1956] has pointed out, this requires that the distribution of income *within* each household be optimal. Given this assumption it is possible to posit the existence of a family utility function. Let $Y_v(t)$ be the income of a vintage v household at time t. The "economic age" of such a household is $t - v$. By definition

$$Y_v(t) = E_v(t) + r_v(t)K_v(t), \tag{1.1}$$

where $K_v(t)$ is wealth, $r_v(t)$ is the after-tax rate of return on wealth, and $E_v(t)$ is the net after-tax earned income of the household.

It will be assumed throughout this book that $r_v(t)$ is the same for every household and for every period of time. A more general model would, of course, introduce a number of complications such as the facts that $r_v(t)$ generally (1) varies over time, (2) is stochastic at any instant of time, (3) can be affected by the household by altering its chosen portfolio. It is shown in the appendix to this chapter that complication 1 presents no real difficulties; the model is readily generalized to allow $r(t)$ to follow any *exogenously given* time path. Complication 3 is eliminated by assuming that there is only one homogeneous asset; hence there are no portfolio decisions to be made. Finally, if there is no portfolio problem, uncertainty (complication 2) can also be handled by a straightforward generalization of the results of this chapter *if* the presence of uncertainty does not change the household's optimal plan. Since the solution of the consumer's lifetime problem under uncertainty is beyond the scope

of this study, I shall restrict myself to the certainty case.[17]   In other
words, the crucial assumption is *not* that r is constant over time; I
assume this only to simplify the exposition. What is crucial is the
assumption that r is *exogenous* to the model, though clearly endogenous to the economic system. This actually consists of two simplifications. First, r is independent of the behavior of any individual
(that is, there are no portfolio choices). And second, r is independent
of the distributions of income and wealth. The latter is the assumption of "no distribution effects" so common in macroeconomics. Of
course, I do not necessarily believe this assumption to be true, nor
even a good approximation. I adopt it only because one cannot
attempt to explain the entire economic system in a single model.
Some things must be left exogenous.

One further comment before leaving this topic. It is obvious that if
a stationary distribution   of wealth is to exist, one of the many
requirements is that the rate of interest be constant through time.
This is another justification for focusing on this case.

Now, returning to (1.1), the wealth $K_v(t)$ of a man of vintage v at
time t depends on (1) his wealth at time v, that is, his inheritance, and
(2) his savings behavior over the past years:

$$K_v(t) = K_v(v) + \int_v^t S_v(\tau)\, d\tau, \tag{1.2}$$

where $K_v(v)$ is his inheritance and $S_v(t)$ is his savings in year t. It will
be convenient at this point to prove that another expression for $K_v(t)$
gives the same value at each point as (1.2). In particular,

$$K_v(t) = K_v(v) e^{r(t-v)} + \int_v^t \{ E_v(\tau) - C_v(\tau) \} e^{r(t-\tau)}\, d\tau, \tag{1.3}$$

where $C_v(\tau)$ is consumption, defined as $Y_v(\tau) - S_v(\tau)$. The proof is
trivial. Differentiate both (1.2) and (1.3) with respect to t to get
$dK_v(t)/dt = S_v(t)$. Then set $t = v$ in both (1.2) and (2.3) and verify
that they both start at $K_v(v)$. Therefore, since the initial value of
$K_v(t)$ and the differential equation defining the path of $K_v(t)$ are
identical in (1.2) and (1.3), both equations must define the same time
path. It will be more convenient to work with (1.3).

To use equation (1.3) it is necessary to know the time paths of both

---

17. In several footnotes in Chapter 2, I indicate where uncertainty would affect the
model. It is suggested there that, for the class of utility functions I shall consider, the
presence of uncertainty does not alter the results in any essential way.

earnings and consumption. In the course of this study, both of these paths will be derived from an explicit maximization process. For the moment, I shall simply take earnings to be exogenous. It remains, then, to select a consumption function. In Chapter 2, assuming earnings to be exogenous, I show that an optimal life-cycle consumption plan for a utility-maximizing household is

$$C_v(t) = C_v(v)e^{g(t-v)}; \quad C_v(v) = f(K_v(v) + M_v), \tag{1.4}$$

where M_v is the lifetime discounted present value of the earnings of a vintage v man,[18] and $f(\cdot)$ and g depend on tastes, the rate of interest, and other parameters.

Substitution of (1.4) into (1.3) yields

$$K_v(t) = e^{r(t-v)}K_v(v) + e^{r(t-v)} \int_v^t E_v(\tau)e^{-r(\tau-v)} d\tau$$
$$- C_v(v) \int_v^t e^{g(\tau-v)} e^{r(t-\tau)} d\tau$$

Finally, defining $M_v(t)$ as the discounted earnings of a vintage v man for the first t periods of his life, this expression can be rewritten:

$$K_v(t) = e^{r(t-v)} \left\{ K_v(v) + M_v(t) - f(K_v(v) + M_v) \frac{1 - e^{-(r-g)(t-v)}}{r-g} \right\}.$$

$$\tag{1.5}$$

Since $K_v(v)$, $M_v(t)$, and M_v are all given, equation (1.5) defines the time path for net worth $K_v(t)$ and substitution into (1.1) yields the time path for income, $Y_v(t)$. If a stationary state exists, all vintages are alike so that only $t - v$, economic age, matters. Defining $A = t - v$, I can write (1.5) for stationary economies as

$$K(A) = e^{rA} \left[K(0) + M(A) - f(K(0) + M) \frac{1 - e^{-(r-g)A}}{r-g} \right]. \tag{1.6}$$

In words, equation (1.6) says that a household's wealth at age A is its inheritance accumulated at compound interest to the present; plus all of its earnings to date, also accumulated to the present; minus a function (which depends on age) of its initial human plus nonhuman wealth.

18. The human capital theorists may call M_v "human wealth" if they please.

From equation (1.6), it is clear what factors determine the stationary distribution of wealth. They are—

1. The *distribution of inheritances*, $K(0)$, which serve as initial conditions in equation (1.6). This distribution is taken to be exogenous in an intragenerational model like the present one, but would be endogenous in an intergenerational model;[19]

2. The *rate of interest*, r, which I also take to be exogenous;

3. The *distribution of lifetime earnings patterns*, $M(A)$, which is the subject of Chapter 3;

4. The *distribution of tastes* which, along with the model of savings developed in Chapter 2, determines the shape of the function $f(\cdot)$ and the value of the constant g;

5. The *rates of income and inheritance taxation*, which enter in ways to be specified in Chapters 2 and 3;

6. The *age distribution* of the population. Since equation (1.6) gives the distribution only within a single age cohort, this information is necessary to derive the overall distribution. If $f_A[K(A)]$ is the density function for wealth in the age A cohort and the fraction of the population with age between A and $A + dA$ is $h(A)dA$, the overall wealth distribution is

$$f_K(K) = \int_0^T h(A)f_A[K(A)]\,dA.$$

If the rate of interest is not constant, so that no stationary distribution exists, the actual wealth distribution at time t depends on 1, 3, 4, 5, and 6 above and also on calendar time t and the entire past history of the interest rate $r(t)$. It is obvious that to say anything about such a distribution very strong assumptions about behavior of $r(t)$ would have to be made. In view of this, and the empirical fact that income distributions appear quite stable over time, I will concentrate on the case where $r(t) = r$ for all t so that a stationary distribution may exist.

It will be noted that in the above list of determinants of $f(K)$ four are "givens" to the present model (ages, tastes, inheritances, and the interest rate), while two are policy variables (tax rates) through which the government might try to affect the distribution. Savings and labor-supply behavior, on the other hand, are endogenous to the model.

19. See Blinder [1973b] for a model determining the distribution of $K(0)$.

1.4 On the Distribution of Labor Incomes

What determines the labor income of a vintage v worker at time t, and why should this quantity vary across individuals? Existing neoclassical microtheory, it would appear, has an answer for this question. Earnings are the product of hours of work times the wage rate. In a competitive system, a person's wage is his marginal product, and for a given wage he optimizes his work effort by equating his marginal rate of substitution between leisure and income to the wage rate. Unfortunately, this analysis is not very informative. In the first place, it is entirely static; and in this study I am very much interested in life-cycle effects. But even more fundamentally, merely stating that the wage is equal to the marginal product only replaces one question with another. Namely, what determines a worker's marginal product, and why does productivity differ among workers?

The two problems are, in fact, intimately related. In static theory, an individual's productivity is a datum of the problem, given exogenously. However, over a longer period of time this productivity becomes endogenous, that is, a matter of individual choice. The entire human-capital literature has been built up around this notion. This suggests that the reason for occupational wage differentials lies in differing tastes, because people with divergent tastes differ in (1) their investment in human capital, and (2) the disutility they attach to each job (along the lines, say, suggested by Tinbergen). For example, Friedman [1962, p. 163] says that to a considerable extent "actual inequality may be the result of arrangements designed to satisfy men's tastes." Of course, this is not the entire story. A worker cannot simply choose any productivity level he likes. He is constrained, perhaps sharply, by his own innate abilities, including the ability to "produce" human capital. Thus, given his tastes and innate abilities, one can visualize each worker as selecting for himself an optimal time path for work, training, and leisure.

These ideas suggest that the "reduced-form" equations for hours of work and wages should have two sets of independent variables: tastes and inheritances of human and nonhuman wealths. Of course, a variety of structural models could conceivably give rise to a reduced form of this type. I shall discuss a possible approach shortly; but first it is worth pausing to make clear what is meant by "inherited human wealth" in an intragenerational income distribution model. This would consist of any abilities that are *exogenous to the household*, including two distinct sorts of attributes: (1) *fixed* attributes, such as

race and sex, and genetically transmitted characteristics such as
"native" intelligence; (2) the worker's initial endowments of variable
attributes, such as education. Category 1 may justifiably be considered exogenous to any model of income distribution. But attributes
in category 2 would clearly be endogenous to an intergenerational
model, being derived from decisions of the parents. One of the more
vexing questions in the theory of income distribution concerns itself
with the intergenerational transmission of inequality via human capital. Some recent studies by Otis Dudley Duncan [1968], Samuel
Bowles [1972], Christopher Jencks et al. [1972], and others have
examined this transmission mechanism empirically. But to my knowledge, there has been no theoretical work on this important problem.

Given this broader definition of inheritance, what sort of structural
model might lead to the reduced-form equations alluded to already?
One possible approach is an extension of Tinbergen's model.

It was shown above how, given a distribution of characteristics
demanded by firms and supplied by individual workers, the solution
of a certain general equilibrium system simultaneously determines
the wage structure, the distribution of earnings, and the allocation of
individuals to jobs. But even this rather complicated model works
only in the very short run. The long-run problem is far more
complex. Even if the difference between long-run and short-run
factor demands from firms is ignored, in the long-run each household
has the opportunity to alter its own skill vector in certain ways, for
example, through training. Thus the Σ vectors, which were *givens* in
the short-run model, must be generated endogenously by the long-
run model. This obviously requires a quite elaborate theory of
investment in human capital.

As the reader will by now have surmised, actual solution of this
long-run general equilibrium model is beyond the scope of this study.
For the present, I shall make the extreme assumption that each
person's productivity is entirely determined for him by his parents, so
that his choices are only over hours of work. This is certainly false,
but it enables the model to approximate closely the wage distribution
of the United States—a useful advantage for simulation purposes.
Hopefully, future research will be able to push much further along
the lines just suggested.

1.5 Simulating the Income Distribution

A basic goal of this monograph is to demonstrate that current
economic theory can indeed tell a great deal about why the distribu-

tion of income under capitalism is the way it is, that is, unequal and skewed. By this I do not mean that, like some of the simple models discussed in Section 1.2, it will imply a specific analytical form for the distribution of income. Reality is far too complex for that. What I do mean is that an economy of individual maximizing units following the models of Chapters 2 and 3, if endowed with certain characteristics similar to those found in the U.S. economy, will indeed produce a distribution of income strikingly like that of the United States, that is, an unequal and highly skewed distribution with a Gini concentration ratio somewhat in excess of 0.40.[20] This may appear to be a tall order for so simple a model, but, I believe, Chapters 4–6 demonstrate that the theory has this capability.

The theory developed in Chapters 2 and 3 is, in a sense, separate and distinct from the uses to which it is put in the simulation studies of Chapters 4–6. Yet there are important interactions, since the theory was specifically designed for simulation purposes. In devising a theoretical model, there is an inevitable trade off between elegance and generality on the one hand, and concrete results on the other. Mathematical reasoning can never extract more information than is embodied in the assumptions. In this book the "generality versus results" trade off has been lopsidedly adjudicated in favor of results. Since the ultimate desire is to simulate the model using real numbers, generality is sacrificed any time it interferes with arriving at an empirically meaningful hypothesis. Chapters 2 and 3 bear the stamp of this methodology in several places. The reader will see where the results of these chapters are amenable to generalization and where they are not.

Appendix 1.1 On Variable Interest Rates

The purpose of this appendix is to demonstrate that the results of the chapter, especially equation (1.5), can be derived even when r is assumed to vary over time in an arbitrary but *exogenous* manner.

Let $r(t)$ be the instantaneous rate of interest at time t. It is clear that $r(t)$ belongs in the definition of income, but that it must be replaced in equation (1.3) and all following expressions by the rate appropriate for accumulating flows at time v up to present value in

---

20. The Gini ratio is the inequality measure associated wth the Lorenz curve. It is equal to twice the area between the actual Lorenz curve and the hypothetical line of perfect equality.

time t:

$$A(t,v) = \exp\left(\int_v^t r(\tau)\,d\tau\right).$$

Note that

$$A(t,t) = 1,$$

and

$$A(T,t)A(t,v) = A(T,v).$$

Similarly, the discount factor used to discount flows at time t to present value at time v is

$$D(t,v) = \frac{1}{A(t,v)}.$$

Using this notation, equation (1.3) is modified to

$$K_v(t) = K_v(v)A(t,v) + \int_v^t \{E(\tau) - C(\tau)\}A(t,\tau)\,d\tau. \tag{1.7}$$

And equation (1.4) is modified to become (this is proved in Chapter 2)

$$C_v(t) = C_0 A(t,v)e^{-\rho(t-v)}, \tag{1.8}$$

where $C_0 = F(K_v(v) + M_v)$. Now, proceeding as in Section 1.3, substitute (1.8) into (1.7) to obtain

$$K_v(t) = K_v(v)A(t,v) + \int_v^t E(\tau)A(t,\tau)\,d\tau$$

$$- F(K_v(v) + M_v)\int_v^t A(t,\tau)A(\tau,v)e^{-\rho(\tau-v)}\,d\tau$$

$$= K_v(v)A(t,v) + \int_v^t E(\tau)\frac{A(t,v)}{A(\tau,v)}\,d\tau$$

$$- F(K_v(v) + M_v)A(t,v)\int_v^t e^{-\rho(\tau-v)}\,d\tau,$$

since $A(t,\tau)A(\tau,v) = A(t,v)$, independent of τ. Thus,

$$K_v(t) = K_v(v)A(t,v) + A(t,v)\int_v^t E(\tau)D(\tau,v)\,d\tau$$

$$- F(K_v(v) + M_v)\frac{1 - e^{-\rho(t-v)}}{\rho}A(t,v).$$

Or, by defining,

$$M_v(t) = \int_v^t E(\tau)D(\tau,v)\,d\tau,$$

this can be written

$$K_v(t) = K_v(v)A(t,v) + M_v(t)A(t,v)$$

$$- A(t,v)F(K_v(v) + M_v)\frac{1 - e^{-\rho(t-v)}}{\rho},$$

which is a precise analog of equation (1.5).

2
A Life-Cycle Model of Consumption and Bequest Behavior

It is futile to try to explain everything economic. The sound procedure is to obtain first utmost precision and mastery in a limited field,
and then to proceed to another, somewhat wider one...

John von Neumann and Oskar Morgenstern

In this chapter I begin to study the optimal behavior of the household over its life cycle.[1] The ultimate goal is to derive for each
household an optimal plan of consumption, capital accumulation,
work, leisure, and an optimal bequest. This is a formidable problem.
As an initial step, I ignore all problems connected with earning
income and assume that the lifetime pattern of earnings is given for
each family. The time path of earnings may be of any arbitrary
shape, so long as it is taken to be independent of consumption
decisions (for the present chapter only). In Section 2.1, the problem is
set up as one of lifetime utility maximization, and some of the basic
assumptions and simplifications are discussed. The next section is
devoted to solving this problem at various levels of generality. In
Section 2.3, I explore some of the properties of the optimal consumption-bequest plan. Since one of the main goals of this study is to
appraise the likely effectiveness of various public policy measures
designed to equalize the income distribution, particular attention is
paid to the effects of variations in the rate of estate taxation. Section
2.4 briefly discusses how the results might be extended to a regime
with progressive estate taxation, and the last section investigates the
present American estate tax in light of the theoretical model. The
chapter has two mathematical appendixes. In the first, I show that
the model can be readily generalized to allow for both a variable

---

1. The words "household" and "consumer" are used interchangeably below.
Throughout this study, I am always referring to a family unity.

interest rate and a variable rate of time preference. The second is devoted to the analytical difficulties involved in allowing the rate of interest to depend on the amount of wealth invested.

The entire analysis is conducted in a framework of perfect certainty and perfect foresight; for example, the individual is assumed to know at the start of his "economic life" the interest rate (or rates) which will prevail over his entire life. Further, the model has only one asset (called "wealth"), so the individual has no portfolio choices.[2] These may appear to be very restrictive assumptions; but recent work in portfolio theory suggests that these simplifications are not crucial and that most of the results would survive translation into a world of uncertainty. In the first place, it has been established both in discrete time[3] and in continuous time[4] that, *for the class of utility functions that I shall consider*, in a many-asset model with uncertain rates of return "the portfolio-selection decision is independent of the consumption decision," [Merton, 1969, p. 252]. Thus, for purposes of the consumption plan, it is *as if* there were only a single asset with a stochastic rate of return. Further, E. S. Phelps [1962] and D. Levhari and T. N. Srinivasan [1969] have demonstrated that the optimal consumption plan in such a one-asset model is essentially identical to the one to be presented here.

2.1 Statement of the Problem

Each family unit is assumed at economic age zero to choose the consumption plan that maximizes its lifetime utility. The family is explicitly assumed to derive utility from bequests. Since I seek fairly strong results, I shall have to make several specific assumptions about the utility functional. To begin with, I assume utility to be additively separable, so that lifetime utility is simply the integral over time of $U(C(t),t)$. This is already somewhat restrictive. Since it makes utility at each instant independent of consumption at any other instant, this form rules out certain intertemporal complementarities that may be quite plausible. However, the objective of this monograph is to obtain specific conclusions about the distributions of income and wealth. To do this I will have to make a number of special assumptions, and this particular one seems one of the least troublesome. Another assump-

2. Of course, the second assumption follows from the first. In a certain world there is really only one asset.
3. See, for example, Samuelson [1969], Hakansson [1970].
4. Merton [1969].

tion inherent in this functional form is that the family derives no satisfaction from the mere possession of wealth, that is, $K(t)$ does not appear in the utility functional.

A third assumption is that tastes are fundamentally the same over time so that instantaneous utility has the special form $U(C(t),t)$ $= U(C(t))e^{-\rho t}$, where ρ is the subjective rate of time discounting. Several remarks are in order. Although tastes probably change endogenously through time, a satisfactory treatment of such changes has not appeared in the literature and an attempt to provide one is beyond the scope of this study. The assumption that time preferences take the form of discounting at a constant rate ρ is in no way essential to the argument; I employ this form only to simplify the exposition. Appendix 2.1 of this chapter shows that the results are readily generalized to accommodate more general time discounting: $U(C(t),t) = U(C(t))R(t)$, where the $R(t)$ are arbitrary discount factors.[5] What *is* esssential is that $R(t)$ is assumed to be independent of $C(t)$.[6]

Now, consider a consumer beginning life at age zero with an inheritance K_0 and ending life with a terminal wealth K_T. This terminal wealth enables him to bequeath an inheritance of $(1-\tau)K_T$ to his heirs. His lifetime utility then takes the form

$$\int_0^T U(C(t))e^{-\rho t}\,dt + B[(1-\tau)K_T], \qquad (2.1)$$

where $B(\cdot)$ is the utility-of-bequest function and τ is the rate of

---

5. Although this is in no way essential to my argument, Robert Strotz [1955-1956] has provided what some feel is a reason for preferring a constant rate of time discounting. He has shown that if a consumer maximizes an integral like $\int_0^T U(C(t))R(t)\,dt$ at time zero, and then has the opportunity to change his plan at a later date, the *only* case in which he will choose *not* to alter his decision is if $R(t) = e^{-\rho t}$. At first blush this "consistency" property (as Strotz calls it) seems quite desirable, especially in a stationary economy where there has been no change in the data between the two decision points. However, Strotz's restrictive form has the undesirable property that the marginal rate of substitution between consumption at time t_1 and consumption at time t_2 depends *only* on the difference t_2-t_1, and not on the value of either. (It also depends, of course, on $C(t_1)$ and $C(t_2)$.) This means, for example, that a 20-year-old looks upon the choice between consumption now versus consumption a year from now in *exactly* the same manner as a 60-year-old. There seems to be no compelling reason why this shoud be so.

6. In two papers, Uzawa [1968a,1968b] has explored the implications of allowing $\rho(t)$ to depend on $U(C(t))$. A different approach to variable time discounting is followed by Goldman [1969].

inheritance taxation.[7] Two basic constraints govern this maximization. First, consumption at each instant is related to savings and income by the instantaneous budget constraint

$$C(t) + s(t) = (1 - u)[E^*(t) + r^* K(t)]$$

$$\equiv E(t) + rK(t), \tag{2.2}$$

where $E(t)$ is labor income after tax, r is the after-tax rate of interest, $E^*(t)$ and r^* are the corresponding before-tax quantities, and u is the rate of proportional income taxation. The second constraint is the obvious one that the change in wealth at each instant is equal to the consumer's saving:

$$\dot{K}(t) = s(t). \tag{2.3}$$

There is an initial condition on the state variable, $K(0) = K_0$, but no terminal condition. Instead, $K(T) = K_T$ is to be selected so as to maximize (2.1).

2.2 The Optimal Consumption-Bequest Plan

To express this problem as a standard problem in optimal control, amenable to treatment by the "maximum principle,"[8] first solve constraint (2.2) for $C(t)$ and substitute the result into the maximand, equation (2.1). Treating (2.3) as the only constraint, define the Hamiltonian function for this problem as

$$H(K,s) = U(E + rK - s)e^{-\rho t} + \mu(t)s,$$

where s is taken to be the control variable, and $\mu(t)$ is the shadow price of capital. Under the assumption of perfect capital markets, $s(t)$ is unconstrained, so, according to Pontryagin's algorithm, first-order conditions are[9]

$$\frac{\partial H}{\partial K} = -\dot{\mu}(t) = rU'(C)e^{-\rho t}, \tag{2.4}$$

7. Throughout this book, T is taken to be known with certainty. However, Yaari [1965] has shown that giving T a *known* probability distribution does not change the results in any essential way *if* the individual can purchase life insurance freely. See also Atkinson [1971b].
8. The maximum principle—also called the minimum principle—is due to Pontryagin and his associates [1962]. The best elementary account for economists is Dorfman [1969], while a more complete account can be found in Bryson and Ho [1969].
9. Since $U(\cdot)$ and $B(\cdot)$ are assumed to be strictly concave, these are also sufficient conditions for a maximum.

$$\frac{\partial H}{\partial s} = - U'(C)e^{-\rho t} + \mu(t) = 0, \tag{2.5}$$

and the transversality condition

$$\mu(T) = \frac{dB[(1-\tau)K_T]}{dK_T} = (1-\tau)B'[(1-\tau)K_T]. \tag{2.6}$$

The reader may have noticed that I have failed to account for the apparent constraint that consumption must always be strictly positive, that is, $C(t) > 0$ for all t. This is because, for the class of utility functions I wish to consider, marginal utility of consumption becomes infinite as C approaches zero; hence solutions with $C(t) = 0$ in some interval could never be optimal. Technically, the assumption that $U'(0) = \infty$ is sufficient to insure an interior maximum throughout.

From (2.4) and (2.5) it is a simple matter to compute the optimal path for consumption. First, take the time derivative of (2.5):

$$- \dot{\mu}(t) = \rho U'(C)e^{-\rho t} - U''(C)e^{-\rho t}\dot{C}.$$

Now equate this to equation (2.4) and solve for $\dot{C}(t)$ to obtain

$$\dot{C} = (r - \rho)\frac{U'(C)}{-U''(C)}. \tag{2.7}$$

This result, which was first reached by Strotz [1955-1956], and later (in more general form) by Yaari [1964], is about as far as one can go with an arbitrary utility function and arbitrary earnings stream.

Note that, since $U''(C)$ is assumed to be negative, (2.7) states that consumption steadily increases if $r > \rho$ and steadily decreases if $\rho > r$. The economic intuition behind this result is as follows. Suppose the household is given just enough money to finance some constant consumption plan for its entire life. If the net rate of interest, $r = r^*(1 - u)$, exceeds the subjective rate of time discounting ρ, it can always increase the value of its lifetime utility integral by deferring consumption and investing its capital at a rate of return r. Hence, the optimal $C(t)$ must be rising over time. Conversely, if ρ exceeds r, the household can improve its position by borrowing at rate r in order to advance its consumption stream toward the present. Thus the optimal $C(t)$ would have to decline over time.

There are two possible ways to proceed from here. If some strong assumptions about the time path of $E(t)$ are made, it may be possible to diagram and analyze the qualitative features of the life cycle in quite general terms.[10] Of course, at this level of generality, not very much can be established. I prefer to pursue an alternative mode of analysis. Specifying the utility function more precisely makes it possible to solve differential equation (2.7) explicitly and analyze the life cycle plan for any arbitrary earnings stream. Such a procedure shows, for example, how the optimal plan depends on the taste parameters of each family.

From the form of (2.7), it is clear that the most convenient case is the class of utility functions for which $U'(C)/U''(C)$ is proportional to C. Fortunately, this class of functions is quite well known in the literature, since it has arisen in several different contexts. In portfolio analysis, such functions are said to display "constant relative risk aversion" according to Pratt's [1964] definition. Since choices involving risk are not at issue here, I shall refer to them simply as iso-elastic utility functions. The general functional form is

$$U(C) = \frac{C^{1-\delta}}{1-\delta} + \text{constant} \qquad \text{for } \delta > 0, \delta \neq 1,$$

$$U(C) = \log C + \text{constant} \qquad \text{for } \delta = 1,$$

(2.8)

where $-\delta$ is the elasticity of marginal utility with respect to consumption. A high value of δ indicates rapidly diminishing returns. These functions have the property that $U'(C)/[-U''(C)] = C/\delta$, so that equation (2.7) simplifies to

$$\frac{\dot{C}}{C} = \frac{r-\rho}{\delta} \equiv g,$$

which has the obvious solution

$$C(t) = C_0 e^{gt}, \tag{2.9}$$

where C_0 is, of course, determined from boundary conditions.

Since the "true" utility function is not known, analytical convenience alone is a powerful argument for adopting the iso-elastic form. However, Yaari [1964] has provided an independent motivation for adopting such a function. In his pioneering paper on optimal lifetime consumption plans, he pointed out an interesting fact. Suppose one believes that the optimal consumption plan should have the following homogeneity property: if lifetime wealth increases, then the optimal $C(t)$ increases *in the same proportion for all t*. In words, any

10. This is done, for example, by Atkinson [1971a].

addition to lifetime purchasing power is distributed across time in the same manner as the original wealth.[11] Yaari has proven that if this plan does not entail equal consumption at every instant, the utility function must be iso-elastic.[12]

Finally, though this fact is not widely recognized, utility function (2.8) has a long and venerable history in macroeconomics, since it is the basis of both Friedman's permanent income model [1957] and the life cycle model of Modigliani and Brumberg [1954]. In fact, as will be made clear shortly, the utility functions behind those models are somewhat less general than the one assumed here.

Given the decision to employ this special functional form, the calculation of the initial level of consumption is easy given the simple relation (1.3) established in Chapter 1:

$$K(t) = K_0 e^{rt} + \int_0^t [E(\tau) - C(\tau)] e^{r(t-\tau)} d\tau.$$

For the special case $t = T$, this becomes

$$K_T - K_0 e^{rT} = \int_0^T [E(t) - C(t)] e^{r(T-t)} dt$$

$$= e^{rT} \int_0^T E(t) e^{-rt} dt - C_0 e^{rT} \int_0^T e^{-rt} e^{gt} dt$$

by equation (2.9). Now define M as the discounted present value (in time-zero dollars) of lifetime net earnings after tax,

$$M \equiv \int_0^T E(t) e^{-rt} dt,$$

and adopt the notation (to be used throughout this book)

$$N(a, T) \equiv \int_0^T e^{-at} dt = \frac{1 - e^{-aT}}{a}.$$

11. This is, of course, a very strong supposition. It rules out, for example, the possibility that a person may be less willing to defer satisfaction when he is poor than when he is rich.

12. There are strong analogies, but only analogies, between the theory of intertemporal choice and the theory of choice under uncertainty by an expected utility maximizer. These analogies have been exploited in a paper by Robert Pollak [1970]. Pollak shows that an appropriate additivity postulate plus an appropriate homogeneity postulate (and I have assumed both) imply that intertemporal choices can *only* be represented by an increasing monotone transformation of one of the iso-elastic utility functions. This theorem provides further justification for assuming (2.8).

Under these definitions, the last equation can be simplified to read

$$K_T - K_0 e^{rT} = M e^{rT} - C_0 e^{rT} N(r-g,T)$$

from which it follows that

$$C_0 = \frac{K_0 + M - K_T e^{-rT}}{N(r-g,T)} \qquad \text{for } \delta \neq 1,$$

$$C_0 = \frac{K_0 + M - K_T e^{-rT}}{N(\rho,T)} \qquad \text{for } \delta = 1. \tag{2.10}$$

Equations (2.9) and (2.10) jointly define the optimal consumption plan. In words, at each instant a certain fraction (which varies with age, tastes, length of life, and the interest rate) of lifetime net wealth is consumed, where lifetime net wealth is defined as the inheritance *plus* the discounted value of lifetime net earnings after tax ("human capital") *minus* the discounted value of the bequest.

Of course, this does not complete the solution since the bequest K_T is not known. However, the transversality condition, equation (2.6), can be used to find K_T in terms of C_0. First, use (2.5) to rewrite (2.6):

$$U'(C_T)e^{-\rho T} = (1-\tau)B'[(1-\tau)K_T]. \tag{2.11}$$

This states that the marginal utility from bequests is just equal to the marginal utility of consumption at death. Since $C_T = C_0 e^{gT}$, equation (2.11) implicitly defines K_T as a function of C_0. In particular, along the locus described by (2.11), it can be shown that the elasticity of K_T with respect to C_0 is simply δ/β, where δ and β are, respectively, the elasticities of $U(\cdot)$ at C_T and $B(\cdot)$ at $(1-\tau)K_T$.[13]

13. *Proof*: Total differentiation of (2.11) gives:

$$\{e^{-\rho T}U''(C_T)e^{gT}\}dC_0 = \{(1-\tau)^2 B''[(1-\tau)K_T]\}dK_T.$$

Dividing through by $U'(C_T)e^{-\rho T} = (1-\tau)B'[(1-\tau)K_T]$ yields

$$\frac{U''(C_T)}{U'(C_T)}dC_0 = (1-\tau)\frac{B''[(1-\tau)K_T]}{B'[(1-\tau)K_T]}dK_T$$

or

$$\frac{dK_T}{dC_0} = \frac{U''/U'}{(1-\tau)B''/B'} = \frac{\delta/C_0}{\beta/K_T}$$

or

$$\frac{C_0}{K_T}\frac{dK_T}{dC_0} = \frac{\delta}{\beta}. \qquad \text{Q.E.D.}$$

Now consider this function in the case of iso-elastic utility, that is, where (2.8) holds and also

$$B(K) = \frac{b^{\beta} K^{1-\beta}}{1-\beta} \qquad \beta > 0,\ \beta \neq 1,$$

(2.12)

$$B(K) = b \log K \qquad \beta = 1,$$

where β is the (constant) elasticity of marginal utility from bequests, and b is a taste parameter indicating the relative preference for bequests versus consumption. Equation (2.11) becomes

$$\frac{e^{-\rho T}}{C_0^{\delta} e^{(r-\rho)T}} = \frac{(1-\tau)b^{\beta}}{(1-\tau)^{\beta} K_T^{\beta}} ;$$

or, solving for K_T,

$$K_T = b(1-\tau)^{(1-\beta)/\beta} e^{(r/\beta)T} C_0^{\delta/\beta}.$$

(2.13)

Equations (2.10) and (2.13) are two implicit equations in initial consumption and the optimal bequest for the iso-elastic case.

In the still more special case where $\delta = \beta$,[14] these equations permit an explicit solution:

$$C_0 = \frac{K_0 + M}{N(r-g,T) + b[(1-\tau)e^{rT}]^{(1-\delta)/\delta}} ,$$

(2.14)

$$K_T = (1-\tau)^{(1-\delta)/\delta} b e^{(r/\delta)T} C_0.$$

(2.15)

In the logarithmic case ($\delta = \beta = 1$), these further simplify to

$$C_0 = \frac{K_0 + M}{N(\rho,T) + b} ,$$

(2.14')

$$K_T = \frac{b e^{rT}(K_0 + M)}{N(\rho,T) + b} .$$

(2.15')

Equation (2.15') shows, for the log case, how the household's optimal bequest— which is positive as long as $b > 0$, that is, as long as bequests have any weight in the utility function—varies with tastes

14. As will be shown below, this further stipulation is necessary to get the Modigliani-Brumberg-Friedman consumption function.

(the parameters b and ρ), the after-tax rate of interest r, its inherited wealth K, and its human wealth M.

2.3 Properties of the Optimal Plan

2.3.1 Comparative Statics of the Optimal Bequest
Consider first the behavior of the optimal bequest as various parameters of the problem change. To begin with, it follows by inspection of equations (2.14)–(2.15) that K_T is homogeneous of degree one in K_0 and M together, but not in K_0 separately.

Proposition 2.1 Under the assumption that $\delta = \beta$, if lifetime disposable wealth of a consumer doubles, his bequest doubles. But if only inherited wealth doubles, his bequest increases by a factor less than two unless he never works.

Since (2.15) shows that the ratio of K_T to C_0 is constant when $\delta = \beta$, it follows immediately that a similar statement holds for the responsiveness of lifetime consumption to K_0. Note that, for these results, there is nothing special about the case $\delta = \beta = 1$.

What about the household's optimal response to a change in the rate of inheritance taxation? Here the logarithmic case is special. A glance at equations (2.14′)–(2.15′) reveals the somewhat surprising result that neither C_0 nor K_T changes in response to variations in τ.

Proposition 2.2 For a household with logarithmic utility, a change in the rate of inheritance taxation does not affect the division of wealth $(K_0 + M)$ between consumption and bequests. Since the bequest is unchanged, the inheritance $(1 - \tau)K_T$ falls by the amount of the tax. That is, the burden of the inheritance tax falls strictly on the heir.

Unfortunately, neither of these propositions generalize to the rest of the iso-elastic family. In particular, the homogeneity result of Proposition 2.1 holds only if $\delta = \beta$; and the nonshifting result of Proposition 2.2 holds only if $\beta = 1$, regardless of the value of δ. The following two propositions can however, be established.

Proposition 2.3 If lifetime disposable wealth $K_0 + M$ increases, the optimal bequest increases more than proportionately, exactly proportionately, or less than proportionately according as β is less than, equal to, or greater than δ. Since lifetime consumption plus the bequest must exhaust disposable resources, precisely the opposite is true of C_0.

Proposition 2.4 The optimal bequest K_T increases, remains the same, or decreases in response to an increase in the inheritance tax τ according as β is greater than, equal to, or less than unity. But in every case the received inheritance $(1 - \tau)K_T$ declines when τ is raised.

Before turning to the proofs of these results, it is worth pausing to consider their intuitive meaning. Proposition 2.3 demonstrates why the Modigliani-Brumberg-Friedman model of the consumption function requires that $\delta = \beta$. If the marginal utility from bequests declines more rapidly than the marginal utility of consumption ($\beta > \delta$), increments to wealth are divided in such a way as to increase the share of consumption. That is, the lifetime average propensity to consume rises. Conversely, if diminishing marginal utility affects consumption more strongly than bequests ($\beta < \delta$), any addition to lifetime wealth is allocated disproportionately in favor of bequests, so that the lifetime average propensity to consume falls. Only in the very special case that $\delta = \beta$ is the lifetime average propensity to consume constant for all wealth levels and thus equal to the marginal propensity to consume.

Proposition 2.4 highlights the borderline nature of the logarithmic utility-of-bequest function. If the marginal utility of leaving a bequest declines faster than the log case ($\beta > 1$), the household responds to higher taxes by increasing its pretax bequest in order to cushion the impact on its posttax bequest. So part of the burden of the tax falls on the testator. Alternatively, if marginal utility declines more slowly than the logarithmic case ($\beta < 1$), the household reduces its bequest when bequests become more expensive to leave. Then more than 100% of the burden of the estate tax falls on the heir. The logarithmic case is the borderline where income and substitution effects just cancel out, leaving no net effect on the testator; the full burden is borne by the heir. Note that these responses are not contingent on the value of δ, the rate at which marginal utility from consumption declines.

I now proceed to the proof of Proposition 2.3.[15] First solve (2.13)

---

15. After writing the first draft of this chapter, I came across an unpublished paper by Sato [1971] which proves propositions like 2.3 and 2.4 for a slightly different model. For a more general treatment, see Atkinson [1971a], which contains proofs of closely related propositions and has been invaluable to me.

for C_0 and substitute the result into (2.10) to obtain a single equation in K_T alone:

$$K_0 + M = K_T e^{-rT} + N(r-g,T)K_T^{\beta/\delta}(1-\tau)^{(\beta-1)/\delta}b^{-\beta/\delta}e^{-(r/\delta)T}.$$

(2.16)

Denoting the sum $K_0 + M$ by the symbol W and taking the derivative of (2.16) with respect to W yields

$$\frac{dK_T}{dW} = \frac{K_T}{K_T e^{-rT} + (\beta/\delta)N(r-g,T)K_T^{\beta/\delta}(1-\tau)^{(\beta-1)/\delta}b^{-\beta/\delta}e^{-(r/\delta)T}},$$

or, using (2.16),

$$\frac{W}{K_T}\frac{dK_T}{dW} = \frac{W}{W + [(\beta/\delta)-1]N(r-g,T)K_T^{\beta/\delta}(1-\tau)^{(\beta-1)/\delta}b^{-\beta/\delta}e^{-(r/\delta)T}}.$$

It follows that the elasticity of K_T with respect to W is unity only when $\beta = \delta$. When $\beta > \delta$, the elasticity is less than unity (and is not constant); if $\beta < \delta$, the elasticity exceeds unity. Since K_T rising *less than proportionately* with W implies necessarily that C_0 rises *more than proportionately*, and vice versa, the proposition is proven.

Proposition 2.4 also follows from (2.16) in a straightforward manner. The implicit derivative with respect to τ is

$$\frac{\partial K_T}{\partial \tau} = \frac{(\beta-1)N(r-g,T)K_T^{\beta/\delta}(1-\tau)^{(\beta-1-\delta)/\delta}b^{-\beta/\delta}e^{-(r/\delta)T}}{\beta N(r-g,T)K_T^{(\beta/\delta)-1}(1-\tau)^{(\beta-1)/\delta}b^{-\beta/\delta}e^{-(r/\delta)T} + \delta e^{-rT}},$$

which has the sign of $\beta - 1$. The second part of the proposition follows by substituting the above formula into the derivative,

$$\frac{\partial[(1-\tau)K_T]}{\partial \tau} = (1-\tau)\frac{\partial K_T}{\partial \tau} - K_T,$$

and simplifying.

2.3.2 A Digression on the Modigliani-Brumberg-Friedman Utility Function

Since the special case where $\delta = \beta$ is so convenient, and since it occupies such a prominent place in the literature, it is worth inquiring whether it has any inherent economic interest. The answer is that if one is willing to accept a plausible story about how tastes for bequests are formed, then one should be willing to accept $\delta = \beta$.[16]

Suppose that the family does not receive utility from the act of giving itself—after all, a bequest is not "given" until after death. Assume instead that the satisfaction comes from the knowledge that the bequest buys consumption for future generations of the family. Suppose further that each generation views its descendants as an infinite-lived family with the same tastes for consumption as its own. This means that the hypothetical infinite family uses its inheritance $(1 - \tau)K_T$ to purchase an infinite consumption stream growing at the rate $g = (r - \rho)/\delta$. Since $(1 - \tau)K_T$ must be the discounted present value of this stream, C_T depends on K_T as follows:

$$(1 - \tau)K_T = \int_T^\infty C_T e^{(g-r)(t-T)} dt = C_T/(r-g), \qquad \text{if } r > g,^{17}$$

or

$$C_T = (r - g)(1 - \tau)K_T.$$

The utility that the descendants derive from this consumption stream, measured in time T utils, is

$$U^* = \frac{1}{1-\delta} \int_T^\infty \left[\{ C_T e^{g(t-T)} \}^{1-\delta} \cdot e^{-\rho(t-T)} \right] dt$$

$$= \frac{C_T^{1-\delta}}{1-\delta} \cdot \frac{1}{\rho - g(1-\delta)} = \frac{C_T^{1-\delta}}{1-\delta} \cdot \frac{1}{r-g}.$$

Combining these two results, the utility which the decedent is buying for his heirs depends on his bequest as follows:

$$U^* = \frac{[(1-\tau)K_T]^{1-\delta}}{1-\delta} \cdot \frac{1}{(r-g)^\delta},$$

16. Since tastes for bequests may be formed in any way, what follows is by no means an argument why β *must* equal δ. Instead, it is a plausible rationale for accepting a conclusion primarily dictated by analytical convenience. Sato [1971] seems to err on this point and is led to ignore cases with $\delta \neq \beta$.

17. Thus one drawback of this story is that it can only be applied when $r > g$, that is, when $\rho > r(1 - \delta)$.

which can be written in discounted utils as

$$B[(1-\tau)K_T] = \frac{b^\delta[(1-\tau)K_T]^{1-\delta}}{1-\delta},$$

where

$$b \equiv \frac{e^{-(r/\delta)T}}{r-g},$$

which is precisely the functional form assumed in (2.12) for the special case when $\beta = \delta$. Note, however, that if this interpretation is accepted, b is *not* an independent taste parameter. Instead, it depends on ρ, δ, T, and r as indicated.

2.3.3 Lifetime Propensities to Consume

Proposition 2.3 highlights the crucial role of the parameters δ and β in determining the portion of total lifetime resources which is consumed. To examine this relationship more closely, note that the definition of lifetime consumption, denoted by C^*, is

$$C^* = C_0 \int_0^T e^{gt} e^{-rt} \equiv C_0 N(r-g, T).$$

By the lifetime budget constraint (2.10),

$$C^* = K_0 + M - K_T e^{-rT}.$$

But, by (2.13), K_T is itself a function of C_0, and therefore of C^*; in particular,

$$C^* = K_0 + M - b[(1-\tau)e^{rT}]^{(1-\beta)/\beta} \left[\frac{C^*}{N(r-g,T)} \right]^{\delta/\beta}.$$

This implicitly defines lifetime consumption C^* as a function of lifetime wealth $K_0 + M = W$ and makes it possible to compute the lifetime marginal and average propensities to spend. Of course, $b = 0$ (that is, no bequest motive) would yield the strict Modigliani-Brumberg [1954] case of unitary lifetime marginal and average propensities to consume. Otherwise, both the lifetime marginal and average propensities to consume are below unity since some part of any increment to wealth is devoted to bequests. In particular, the marginal propensity to consume (MPC) is

$$\frac{dC^*}{dW} = \frac{1}{1 + (b\delta/\beta)[(1-\tau)e^{rT}]^{(1-\beta)/\beta}N(r-g,T)^{-\delta/\beta}C^{*(\delta/\beta)-1}} < 1.$$

This expression also reveals that whether the marginal propensity to spend out of wealth is increasing or decreasing depends upon the relative magnitudes of δ and β. If $\delta = \beta$, the lifetime MPC is constant over all wealth levels. If $\delta > \beta$, the MPC falls with increasing wealth; and if $\delta < \beta$, it rises. This, of course, accords with intuition as well as with the results in Proposition 2.3 on the *average* propensity to consume.

The relationship between δ and β thus acquires considerable importance for the effect of income distribution on the macro savings function and thus for the trade off (if any) between income inequality and growth. If $\delta = \beta$, the conventional assumption in macroeconomics of "no distribution effects" is correct, and there is no trade off. Anti-equality arguments[18] have often cited the potential ill effects of egalitarian redistribution on aggregate savings. If $\delta > \beta$, there is something to this argument and a trade off between equality and growth actually exists; if $\delta < \beta$ the reverse is true. I shall investigate this question in some simulation experiments in Chapter 4.

2.4 A Note on Progressive Taxation

The model has been constructed under the assumption that the inheritance tax is proportional. Among other things, this makes it possible to ignore the difference between inheritance taxes and estate taxes. However, in reality, almost all death duties are progressive. This section considers how household behavior might be affected by a progressive estate tax of the kind currently imposed by the federal government.

Observe first that the determination of the optimal lifetime consumption plan—with the exception of the initial level C_0—is independent of any bequest considerations.[19] In particular, even under a

18. See, for example, Wallich [1960, pp. 122–125, 131–132].
19. This conclusion, in fact, holds in a much broader context than the present one. In a certainty model, equation (2.7) uniquely determines the time path of $C(t)$, except for C_0, independently of bequest considerations. The latter, in turn, determine C_0. Yaari [1965] has shown that if time of death is *uncertain*, but life insurance is available, the consumption and bequest decisions remain separable in this sense. But this is not true if insurance is unavailable.

progressive estate tax the family has an optimal consumption plan that grows exponentially at a rate g. The general condition for the optimal bequest is that the marginal utility of bequest be equal to the marginal utility of deathbed consumption:

$$U'(C_T)e^{-\rho T} = \frac{dB[\phi(K_T)]}{dK_T},$$

where $\phi(K_T) \equiv K_T[1 - \tau(K_T)]$ is a concave function giving the after-tax estate corresponding to each before-tax bequest. Performing this computation for the iso-elastic case and simplifying yields the condition

$$e^{-(r/\beta)T}\phi(K_T) = bC_0^{\delta/\beta}\phi'(K_T)^{1/\beta}. \tag{2.17}$$

If equation (2.13) is solved for C_0 and the result is substituted into (2.17), K_T can be expressed as an implicit function of K_0, M, and other parameters. In general, equation (2.17) cannot be solved explicitly; but in the logarithmic case ($\beta = \delta = 1$), it may be possible to do so. If $\beta = \delta = 1$, equation (2.17) becomes (after multiplying both sides by K_T)

$$K_T e^{-rT} = \frac{bC_0 K_T \phi'(K_T)}{\phi(K_T)}.$$

Now if ϕ has constant elasticity equal to η ($0 < \eta < 1$), this can be solved explicitly with the aid of equation (2.14'):

$$K_T = \frac{b\eta e^{rT}(K_0 + M)}{N(\rho, T) + b\eta} \tag{2.18}$$

which is similar to equation (2.15').[20] Thus, under these restrictive functional forms, a person with taste parameter b facing a flat-rate estate tax behaves exactly like a person with a greater taste for bequests (b/η) facing a progressive tax structure.

Straightforward calculations using equation (2.18) show that the particular kind of tax progression considered here (lowering η below unity)—

20. By comparing (2.18) with (2.15'), the reader will observe that adding progression—in this particular form—to the tax structure turns out to be equivalent to lowering the taste for bequests. That is, replacing the taste parameter b with $b\eta < b$ in equation (2.15'). This result is due to the particular functional forms chosen. The utility-of-bequest function was taken to be $b\log(\phi)$. Assuming further that (except for a constant) $\phi = K^\eta$ leads to a utility-of-bequest function $b\log(K^\eta) = b\eta\log(K)$.

1. reduces the optimal level of bequests corresponding to any given values of the other parameters;
2. does not affect the elasticity of K_T with respect to wealth;
3. lowers the elasticity of K_T with respect to the taste parameter b.

Finally, it is easily established that the elasticity of K_T with respect to η is less than unity for any positive η and approaches unity as η approaches zero. That is, increases in the degree of progression of the estate tax have a *less than proportionate* impact on the level of bequests. Further, this elasticity depends on tastes, but is *independent of wealth* (that is, independent of $K_0 + M$). Thus, adding progression to the rate structure reduces each bequest by a *percentage* that depends on tastes (it falls with higher b) but not on wealth. It therefore seems plausible that the distribution of before-tax bequests would be *slightly more* concentrated under progressive estate taxation than under a proportional tax. "More" because families with a very strong taste for bequests will not be much deterred by the progressive rates. "Slightly" because the rich will not react to progression any more dramatically than the poor.

Before leaving this subject, it is worth pausing to consider what type of progressive tax structure would give rise to the analytically convenient $\phi(K_T)$ function with constant elasticity, and whether the U.S. estate tax actually conforms to this model.[21] First, if $\phi(K_T) \equiv K_T[1 - \tau(K_T)] = mK_T^\eta$, where $\tau(K_T)$ is the effective tax rate on an estate of K_T, and m is a constant, then (omitting the subscript T for convenience) $\tau(K) = 1 - mK^{\eta-1}$. This function is depicted in Figure 2.1.

Effective tax rate, τ

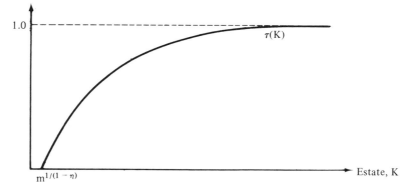

Figure 2.1 A theoretical progressive tax function

21. The U.S. estate tax is considered in more detail in the following section.

One interesting property of this functional form is that although $\tau(K)$ always rises with K, the *elasticity* of $\tau(K)$ with respect to K is always *declining*. In other words, a given percentage increment in estate size leads to a smaller and smaller percentage increment in the effective tax rate as K rises, so that for very high estates the tax is very nearly proportional. This can be proven directly. By definition,

$$\eta \equiv \frac{K\phi'(K)}{\phi(K)} = \frac{1 - \tau(K) - K\tau'(K)}{1 - \tau(K)} = 1 - \frac{K\tau'(K)}{1 - \tau(K)}$$

so that

$$\left[\frac{\tau(K)}{1 - \tau(K)}\right]\left[\frac{K\tau'(K)}{\tau(K)}\right] = 1 - \eta, \qquad\qquad \text{a constant.}$$

Now, under rate progression the first term in square brackets rises as K rises. Therefore, the second term must fall; and in the limit as $\tau \to 1$, the elasticity must approach zero. One of the notable characteristics of the actual American estate tax is that the elasticity of the effective tax rate is, in fact, a declining function of estate size, falling approximately to zero in the uppermost brackets.[22]

It remains to consider how well the tax structure implicit in the functional form $\phi(K_T) = mK_T^\eta$ actually fits the facts. From data on U.S. estate tax returns (given in Table 2.1) the following functional forms were fitted by ordinary least squares:

$$\text{tax} = a + b(K_T), \qquad\qquad (2.19\text{a})$$

$$\text{tax} = b(K_T - \$60{,}000), \qquad\qquad (2.19\text{b})$$

$$\text{tax} = aK_T^b, \qquad\qquad (2.19\text{c})$$

$$\text{tax} = a(K_T - \$60{,}000)^b, \qquad\qquad (2.19\text{d})$$

$$\phi(K_T) \equiv K_T - \text{tax} = mK^\eta. \qquad\qquad (2.19\text{e})$$

The \$60,000 term in equations (2.19b) and (2.19d) forces the constant to be the one implied by the \$60,000 exemption. Although all five specifications fit the sixteen data points quite well, the best-fitting functional form was (2.19e)—the one mentioned in the theoretical discussion above. The point estimate of the elasticity η was 0.932, indicating mild progression. The standard error of 0.004, and the R^2

22. See Table 2.1.

for the equation of 0.9998, indicate that the results have a considerable degree of precision. In particular, the null hypothesis of no rate progression ($\eta = 1$) can be summarily rejected at any level of significance.

2.5 The Federal Estate Tax

It may be useful at this point to consider briefly the structure of the death duties actually imposed in the United States. Unfortunately, these duties are a complex agglomeration of state and federal taxes which do not fit neatly into any theoretical framework. The purpose of this section is to get some idea of the *magnitude* of the estate tax, its degree of *progression*, and its *economic effects*.

Death duties in the United States come in three parts (ignoring the special treatment accorded to trusts). The federal government levies an estate tax of the kind I have been considering in the theoretical model. However, the tax is progressive: the first $60,000 bequeathed is exempt from taxation, and marginal rates are graduated upwards from a beginning rate of 3% on the first $5,000 of taxable estate to a top rate of 77% on the amount in excess of $10,000,000. All but one of the states (Nevada is the lone exception) levy an inheritance tax, and most of these are also progressive. The rates here, however, are graduated according to the individual heir's inheritance. Also, the federal government allows a credit (up to a stipulated maximum) for state inheritance taxes paid. Finally, there is a federal tax on gifts *inter vivos* which, as one might expect, does not conform to the theoretical model of a gift tax fully integrated with the estate tax. Instead, the rates are three-quarters of the corresponding estate tax rates, and there are both lifetime exemptions and annual exclusions. Despite the favorable treatment accorded to gifts *inter vivos*, decedents have not taken full advantage of these tax loopholes. This has puzzled students of the estate and gift taxes.[23] Since the state taxes differ so widely, in what follows I consider only the federal tax.[24]

---

23. See Shoup [1966, p. 17-25], and Fiekowsky [1956].
24. As an example of state inheritance taxation, the tax in California is graduated both by size of inheritance and relation to the deceased. The lowest rates apply to minor children. The first $12,000 is exempt from taxation, and the rates rise from 2% to 10% after that. The highest rates are applied to "strangers in blood" who may receive only $50 free of tax. Marginal rates for them graduate upward from 10% to 24%. (See Somers [1965, Table 1, p. 13].) Gift tax rates and exemptions for gifts "made in contemplation of death" are identical to inheritance tax rates and exemptions [Somers, 1965, p. 17].

Table 2.1 presents the most recent available data on federal estate tax collections, by size of estate. Column 1 lists the various brackets for *gross estate*, which includes all the decedent's assets without deductions for outstanding debts. Column 2 lists the average *economic estate* in each bracket. A decedent's "economic estate" is, roughly, his net worth at death, and corresponds most closely with the variable K_T used in the model. Column 3 gives the average estate tax paid by an estate falling in each bracket. To a good degree of approximation, this is the tax paid on the average estate; so column 4 provides an "effective tax rate" in each bracket, defined by dividing the average tax bill by the average economic estate. Columns 5 and 6 are offered so the reader can compare the effective rates with the nominal rates built into the tax law. In column 5, I present the "hypothetical" tax rate which the average estate in each bracket *would have paid* were there no deductions other than the marital deduction, but the maximum credit for state taxes was taken. Column 6 gives the marginal tax rate applicable to the average economic estate under these same assumptions. The salient facts apparent from even a quick perusal of Table 2.1 are as follows.

1. The effective tax rates are quite low, far lower than the "equivalent" income tax rates.[25]

2. The effective rates are in fact progressive, although deductions make them proportional in the very highest bracket. One might wonder how much of this progressivity is due to the $60,000 exemption, and how much is due to the graduated rates. A crude calculation I have made suggests that just over 60% of the total progressivity of the tax structure is attributable to the exemption, with the rest attributable to graduated marginal rates. The hypothesis that there is no effective rate progression—that all the progressivity comes from exempting the first $60,000—is easily rejected at any significance level.[26]

---

25. To find the income tax bracket roughly equivalent to each estate tax bracket, divide by 15.5—the approximate present value at a 6% rate of discount of an annuity of $1 per year for an entire 47-year working life.

26. The crude calculation is as follows. In order to get a single number to represent progressivity, I force the tax structure to have constant elasticity. That is, I fit an equation of the form $\text{tax} = a(K_T)^b$. The amount by which b exceeds unity is a plausible measure of progressivity. Performing this calculation on U.S. data from Table 2.1 yields a point estimate of b equal to 1.679, with standard error 0.124. (The R^2 for the equation was 0.934.) Now, to see if this observed progressivity is really attributable to the exemption, I fit a tax structure of the form $\text{tax} = a(K_T - \$60,000)^b$. If the exemption were really the only source of progression, the value of b should fall to unity. The amount by which it exceeds unity is a measure of the progressivity inherent in the graduated rates *alone*. A regression on U.S. data yields a point estimate 1.259, with

TABLE 2.1 EFFECTIVE VERSUS NOMINAL ESTATE TAX RATES (1969)

Gross Estate Bracket (1)	Ave. Econ. Estate (2)	Ave. Tax Bill (3)	Effective Rate (4)	Hypothetical Rate (5)	Marginal Rate (6)
$60,000–$70,000	$ 65,133	288	0.4%	0.2%	7%
$70,000–$80,000	70,175	329	0.5%	0.7%	11%
$80,000–$90,000	78,283	1,164	1.5%	1.8%	11%
$90,000–$100,000	86,494	2,163	2.5%	2.9%	14%
$100,000–$120,000	99,208	3,935	4.0%	4.7%	18%
$120,000–$150,000	123,051	5,722	4.7%	7.6%	27.2%
$150,000–$200,000	154,324	9,896	6.4%	12.1%	26.4%
$200,000–$300,000	211,361	20,069	9.5%	16.4%	27.6%
$300,000–$500,000	324,133	42,916	13.2%	20.3%	28.8%
$500,000–$1 million	561,908	94,346	16.8%	23.8%	31%
$1 million–$2 million	1,086,630	220,609	20.3%	27.4%	33.4%
$2 million–$3 million	1,865,979	444,996	23.8%	30.9%	37.8%
$3 million–$5 million	2,869,907	756,810	26.4%	34.6%	44.2%
$5 million–$10 million	5,096,669	1,358,851	26.7%	41.0%	55.8%
$10 million and over	13,992,814	3,742,756	26.7%	53.0%	61%
All taxable estates	$236,983	$32,111	13.6%	17.6%	27.6%

Sources:
Column 1: U.S. Internal Revenue Service, *Statistics of Income—1969, Estate Tax Returns*, Table 8, p. 20.
Columns 2–3: Calculated from *ibid.*, Table 8.
Column 4: Column 3 divided by column 2.
Columns 5–6: Calculated from Tables A and B of Estate Tax Return, *ibid.*, p. 47.

3. The many deductions (for funeral and administrative expenses, contributions to charity, and other reasons) cause a serious erosion of the estate tax base, at least for estates above $120,000, but have only a mild effect on total progressivity. The large "slippage" attributable to the deductions is revealed in the table by comparing column 5—the effective rates that would have prevailed in the absence of all deductions except the marital deduction—with column 4. It is clear that these deductions are worth relatively little to estates below $120,000 but reduce the tax liability of large fortunes dramatically. Yet the overall progressivity inherent in the actual effective rates is only slightly less than the progressivity implied by the hypothetical rate.[27]

There is one other question worth investigating. Since the rich have a far greater incentive to make use of the generous provisions for gifts *inter vivos*,[28] is it possible that this is enough to destroy the progressivity of federal death duties taken as a whole? There is very little data on the combined lifetime gift and estate taxes paid by individuals. We can, however, make use of one of the special studies made by the Department of the Treasury on this question. One such study was based on 1959 returns (mainly people who died in 1958). Earlier gift tax returns of a sample of 1959 estate-tax filers were traced to arrive at a total lifetime "gross transfer" (gifts plus estate). The results of this study are presented in Table 2.2. It should be clear from this table that gift taxation does not alter greatly the progressivity of the structure of federal death duties.[29]

What are the economic effects of the estate tax? The theoretical model of this chapter suggests that an increase in a *proportional* estate tax can increase or decrease lifetime consumption and before-tax

standard error 0.025. (R^2 for the equation was 0.995.) The null hypothesis that $b = 1$ is rejected at any level of significance. The comments in the text are based on the idea that the exemption accounts for $(0.679 - 0.259)/0.679 = 62\%$ of the total progressivity.

27. This assertion is based on a crude calculation similar to that explained in the previous footnote. Fitting a functional form $tax = a(K_T)^b$ to the *hypothetical* estate tax led to a point estimate for b of 1.756 with standard error 0.154. This indicates a slightly higher degree of progressivity than the actual tax returns show, but the difference is not great. Similarly, fitting the functional for $tax = a(K_T - \$60,000)^b$ to the hypothetical tax structure results in an estimated b equal to 1.332 with standard error 0.034, which again does not differ much from the corresponding estimate from the actual tax data.

28. This is documented by Fiekowsky [1956], who also shows that they in fact make remarkably little use of these tax loopholes.

29. The fact that these effective rates often *exceed* the effective rates on estate taxes considered alone makes one suspicious about the accuracy of the Treasury's special study. Since gift tax rates are lower, any "weighted average" of gift tax rates and estate tax rates must be less than the latter.

bequests but must diminish the after-tax inheritances received by heirs. Furthermore, it was shown that if utility functions are logarithmic, the tax induces no change in behavior so that heirs bear the full burden of the tax and there is no deadweight loss. How does this square with the (scanty) available evidence on consumer responses to a *progressive* estate tax?

First, there is substantial agreement (based, it would seem, on casual empiricism) that death duties are *relatively* nondistorting as compared with alternative sources of revenue. According to one student of federal tax policy, "death taxes have less adverse effects on incentives than income taxes of equal yield."[30] The best studies of the economic effects of death duties known to me are by Seymour Fiekowsky [1956, 1966] and Carl Shoup [1966].[31] The following two paragraphs summarize their conclusions.

Death taxes affect two classes of people, potential decedents and heirs. The effect on heirs is clear enough. An increase in estate taxation means a loss of wealth with no countervailing substitution effect. There is a presumption, therefore, that the tax induces greater work effort and/or restricts consumption. Further, all available evi-

TABLE 2.2 EFFECTIVE TAX RATES ON TOTAL
GROSS TRANSFERS (1959)

Size of Gross Transfer	Effective Gift-Estate Tax Rate
Under $100,000	0.9%
$100,000–$200,000	6.0%
$200,000–$300,000	11.0%
$300,000–$500,000	14.8%
$500,000–$1 million	18.7%
$1 million–$2million	23.0%
$2 million–$3 million	24.2%
$3 million–$5 million	27.2%
$5 million–$10 million	31.1%
$10 million and over	28.0%

Source: Calculated from data in Table E-10, p. 227, in Shoup [1966].

30. Pechman [1966, p. 179].
31. See also Harold Somers [1965].

dence suggests that "in practice the tax results in little if any increase in income through extra work" [Shoup, pp. 97–98] because recipients of taxable estates are mainly very wealthy individuals. It is quite conceivable, however, that in the absence of the $60,000 exemption the incentive effects on heirs to smaller fortunes might be considerable.

The effects on the behavior of potential testators is much more complex. Both income and substitution effects are present. To the extent that lifetime consumption and bequests are alternative uses of wealth, the substitution effect of higher inheritance taxes leads to lower bequests and higher lifetime consumption. Income effects, however, may spoil this neat picture. An increase in the inheritance tax, if bequests enter the utiliy function at all, represents a diminution of lifetime real income. Whether the consumer reacts by cutting back on lifetime consumption or reducing his bequest depends on the relative income elasticities of the two "goods." If we think of the motive for leaving an estate as insuring an adequate consumption level for one's heirs, imposition of an estate tax might even lead decedents to increase their bequests. This is especially likely at high wealth levels, where the marginal utility of additional consumption is low. In practice, for those large fortunes covered by the estate tax, "the *prospect* of death duties has had a negligible effect upon accumulation incentives" [Shoup, p. 229]. This is, perhaps, attributable to the low marginal utility of *both* consumption *and* bequests at such high wealth levels. By contrast, the motivation for decedents who leave smaller bequests to provide support for their survivors seems strong. For such people—most of whom are exempt from the present tax—an estate tax could well provide an incentive to accumulate more capital in order to preserve their after-tax estate.

These remarks, of course, are precisely what is indicated by the theoretical model. It was stated in Section 2.3 that a family would respond to the tax by restricting lifetime consumption and adding to the before-tax bequest if the marginal utility function was elastic. However, this effect could never be strong enough to lead to an increased level of after-tax bequests. By contrast, if the marginal utility function were inelastic, the response would be to substitute consumption for bequests. The restrictive functional form with which I have worked seems sufficiently flexible to account for any of the behavioral patterns mentioned by Fiekowsky and Shoup, even with a proportional tax. Further, as was shown in Section 2.4, the American progressive estate tax can be treated as a proportional tax by suitable reinterpretation of one taste parameter. Therefore, in the simulation studies of Chapters 4-6, I will simplify things by supposing that the federal estate tax is proportional.

As has been stated, in practice the estate tax seems to induce little change in behavior on the part of potential decedents. To explain this, Fiekowsky and Shoup have suggested that real consumption and consumption by one's heirs are *not* the arguments of the family utility function.[32] Instead, they suggest, lifetime utility of wealthy individuals probably depends more on wealth holdings during life. If this is so, since no estate tax is levied on wealth held before death, it has no effect on their behavior. While not denying that people may in fact derive utility from the power and prestige of large accumulations of wealth, I would point out that such a hypothesis is *not necessary* to explain the observed insensitivity of individual behavior to death duties. As shown above, if individual utility functions are approximately logarithmic, the estate tax elicits no behavioral response.

Appendix 2.1 Optimal Consumption with Variable Interest Rate and Variable Time Preference

In reality, there is no good reason to assume that the family's rate of time discounting is constant over its lifetime. Similarly, the rate of interest also varies over time. Furthermore, owing to various tax loopholes, indivisibilities in financial markets and the like, the rich earn a better return on capital than the poor. Analytically, these remarks suggest that the model should be amended to allow for an arbitrary time discounting function $\rho(t)$ and an interest rate that depends both on time and the amount of capital invested, $r = r(t, K)$ with $\partial r / \partial K > 0$. This most general case is hopelessly complicated, but in two interesting special cases some results can be established. This appendix takes up the case where both the rate of time discounting and the interest rate follow arbitrary *but exogenous* time paths over the consumer's lifetime. It will be shown that these generalizations present no new analytical difficulties, so that all of the results of this chapter continue to hold with only trivial modifications. I have chosen to deal with the simpler case of a constant r and ρ in the text only to simplify the notation and because the case where $r(t)$ is constant over time is compatible with the existence of a stationary distribution.

32. See Shoup [1966, pp. 90–91] and Fiekowsky [1966, pp. 231-234].

In Appendix 2.2 I discuss the case where $r = r(K)$, with $r'(K) > 0$. This special case has the advantage of being consistent with steady-state income and wealth distributions. However, it will be shown that only some of the results will go through to this case.

I now turn to the case where r and ρ vary exogenously through time. To simplify the notation, define the accumulation factor from time 0 to time t as in Appendix 1.1:

$$A(t,0) = \exp\left(\int_0^t r(\tau) d\tau \right)$$

and, correspondingly, the discount factor from time t to time 0 as

$$D(t,0) = \exp\left(-\int_0^t r(\tau) d\tau \right).$$

With these definitions, two obvious relations hold:

$$A(t,0)D(t,0) = 1 \tag{2.20}$$

$$A(T,t)A(t,0) = A(T,0). \tag{2.21}$$

Similarly, instead of a constant rate of time preference ρ define arbitrary time preference factors $R(t)$ to be applied to consumption at age t. In this notation the *instantaneous rate of time preference* $\rho(t)$ is

$$\rho(t) \equiv -\frac{\dot{R}(t)}{R(t)}.$$

Now the family's lifetime problem is to maximize

$$\int_0^T U[C(t)]R(t) dt + B[(1-\tau)K_T]$$

subject to the boundary condition $K(0) = K_0$ and the equations

$$C(t) = r(t)K(t) + E(t) - s(t),$$

$$\dot{K}(t) = s(t).$$

Proceeding as in Section 2.2 above, the Hamiltonian is

$$H(K,s,t) = U[E + r(t)K - s]R(t) + \mu(t)s,$$

from which the first-order conditions follow:

$$\frac{\partial H}{\partial K} = r(t) U'(C) R(t) = -\dot{\mu}(t),$$

$$\frac{\partial H}{\partial s} = -U'(C) R(t) + \mu(t) = 0.$$

Using the second equation to find an expression for $\dot{\mu}(t)$, and equating this to the first equation yields

$$\dot{R}(t) U'(C) + R(t) U''(C) \dot{C} = -r(t) R(t) U'(C).$$

Solving for $\dot{C}$ leads to an equation analogous to equation (2.7) in the text:

$$\dot{C} = \left[r(t) + \frac{\dot{R}(t)}{R(t)} \right] \frac{U'(C)}{-U''(C)}$$

$$= [r(t) - \rho(t)] \frac{U'(C)}{-U''(C)}.$$

The only difference is that $r(t)$ and $\rho(t)$ are now (known) functions of time instead of constants. If the utility function is logarithmic, the explicit solution of this differential equation (which, of course, no longer implies a constant growth rate for consumption) is

$$C(t) = C_0 \exp\left(\int_0^t \{ r(\tau) - \rho(\tau) \} \, d\tau \right)$$

which, in the present notation, can be written

$$C(t) = C_0 A(t,0) R(t), \tag{2.22}$$

which is an exact analog of equation (2.9). From here on I shall restrict my attention to this special case.

Following the procedures of Section 2.2, the initial level of consumption is determined as follows:

$$K_T - K_0 A(T,0) = \int_0^T [E(t) - C(t)] A(T,t)\, dt$$

$$= \int_0^T [E(t) - C(t)] \frac{A(T,0)}{A(t,0)}\, dt \qquad \text{by (2.21)}$$

$$= A(T,0) \int_0^T [E(t) - C(t)] D(t,0)\, dt \qquad \text{by (2.20)}.$$

Defining $M \equiv \int_0^T E(t) D(t,0)\, dt$, and substituting this definition along with (2.21) into the last expression, yields

$$K_T - K_0 A(T,0) = A(T,0)M - A(T,0)C_0 \int_0^T R(t)\, dt \qquad \text{by (2.20)}$$

$$\equiv A(T,0)M - A(T,0)C_0 \cdot P,$$

where $P \equiv \int_0^T R(t)\, dt$. Solving this last equation for C_0 yields

$$C_0 = \frac{K_0 + M - K_T D(T,0)}{P} \tag{2.23}$$

which is a direct analog of equation (2.10) for the logarithmic case. Substitution of (2.23) into (2.22) gives the optimal consumption path in terms of initial wealth, terminal wealth, and lifetime discounted earnings:

$$C(t) = \frac{A(t,0)R(t)}{P} [K_0 + M - K_T D(T,0)] \tag{2.24}$$

which can be considered as a function

$$C(t) = a(t,\ldots)[K_0 + M - K_T D(T,0)],$$

where the constants $a(\ldots)$ now depend on the complete time path of interest rates $r(t)$ and time preference rates $\rho(t)$. This is why an economy where $r(t)$ changes over time *cannot have a stationary wealth distribution*, but an economy where $\rho(t)$ changes over time still can (though it becomes increasingly implausible). When $r(t)$ varies over time, the constant $a(\dots)$ *depends on calendar time*; therefore, no stationary distribution can exist. By contrast, $\rho(t)$ varies only by age and that means that the constants $a(\dots)$ *depend on the household's age.* Therefore, as long as the age distribution of the population is constant and there is a constant distribution of tastes, a steady-state wealth distribution remains possible.[33]

To determine the optimal bequest and initial level of consumption, I again appeal to the transversality condition,

$$R(T)U'(C_T) = \frac{dB[(1-\tau)K_T]}{dK_T}$$

or, in the logarithmic case,

$$\frac{R(T)}{C_0 A(T,0)R(T)} = \frac{b}{K_T},$$

which has the solution

$$K_T = bA(T,0)C_0. \tag{2.25}$$

Substitution of (2.25) into (2.23) yields the initial level of consumption,

$$C_0 = \frac{K_0 + M}{P + b}, \tag{2.26}$$

which is the obvious analog of equation (2.14′). Finally, (2.25) and (2.26) together imply

$$K_T = \frac{bA(T,0)(K_0 + M)}{P + b}$$

which is the analog of (2.15′).

33. Of course, a "constant distribution of tastes" means much more here than it does when ρ is constant. When ρ is constant, we only have to assume that the distribution of ρ is unchanged over time; that is, at each instant the ρ's of those "being born" are distributed in the same way as the ρ's of those dying. When $\rho(t)$ depends on age, we need the stronger assumption that the distribution of $\rho(t)$ functions is the same in every age cohort.

Appendix 2.2 Optimal Consumption with an Endogenous Interest Rate

I now return to the simpler model where the rates of interest and time preference are constant through time. Appendix 2.1 has shown that this involved no essential loss of generality.

One way to make the rate of interest facing each individual an endogenous variable (that is, one that the consumer himself can influence) is to suppose that it depends on the amount of wealth invested: $r = r(K(t))$. I shall think of $r'(K)$ as positive, but the reader may think of it as negative if he prefers. Since the optimization problem is by now (painfully?) familiar, I shall run through the calculations without much comment.

To maximize: $\int_0^T U[C(t)]e^{-\rho t}\}t + B[1-\tau)K_T]$ subject to $K(0) = K_0$, $C(t) = E(t) + r(K)K(t) - s(t)$, and $\dot{K} = s$. The Hamiltonian is

$$H(K,s,t) = U[E + r(K)K - s]e^{-\rho t} + \mu(t)s,$$

so first-order conditions are

$$\frac{\partial H}{\partial K} = e^{-\rho t}U'(C)[r(K) + r'(K)K] = -\dot{\mu}(t),$$

$$\frac{\partial H}{\partial s} = -e^{-\rho t}U'(C) + \mu(t) = 0.$$

It follows from these that

$$\rho e^{-\rho t}U'(C) - e^{-\rho t}U''(C)\dot{C} = e^{-\rho t}[r(K) + r'(K)K]U'(C),$$

or, solving for $\dot{C}$,

$$\dot{C} = [r'(K)K + r - \rho]\frac{U'(C)}{-U''(C)}.$$

With the logarithmic utility function,

$$\frac{\dot{C}}{C} = r'(K)K + r(K) - \rho = r(K)\left[\frac{dr}{dK}\frac{K}{r} + 1\right] - \rho.$$

This differential equation describing the time path of consumption, in its general form, is analytically intractable. Only in one very special case can it be solved readily. This is the case where $r[(dr/dK)(K/r) + 1] = a$, a constant. What functional form does this imply for

$r(K)$? The answer is easily obtained by integration. If

$$\frac{dr}{dK}\frac{K}{r} = \frac{a-r}{r}$$

then

$$\frac{dr}{a-r} = \frac{dK}{K}$$

so that

$$-\log(a-r) = \log K + \text{constant},$$

$$\frac{1}{a-r} = hK,$$

$$r = a - \frac{1}{hK},$$

where h is some constant. This particular $r(K)$ function is illustrated in Figure 2.2. If it should, by chance, approximate the way the interest rate varies with K (in the relevant range), then the differential equation would have the obvious solution

$$C(t) = C_0 e^{\gamma t}, \qquad \text{where } \gamma \equiv a - \rho.$$

So this much of the model would go through. However, even in this very special case, as the reader may readily verify, the steps by which C_0 was determined cannot easily be performed. Since everything else

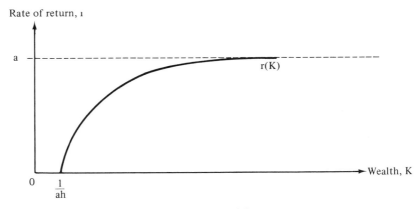

Figure 2.2 A possible relationship between r and k

depends on calculating C_0, the case where r depends on K must remain a desirable but impracticable generalization.

Before leaving this topic, the reader should note that there are strong analogies between the problem of this chapter and the well-known "Ramsey problem" of optimal growth theory. The return on wealth, $r(K)K$, is a kind of "production function" for the individual. With an iso-elastic utility function and a linear production function $f(K) = rK$ the problem was easily solved. Introducing nonlinearities into the production function, however, normally makes it impossible to get a closed analytical result. The particular relation between $r(K)$ and K given above turns out to be the only nonlinearity that can be readily handled. The reason is simple enough: if the production function is $f(K) = r(K)K$, then the particular relation $r = a - 1/hK$ implies a production function $f(K) = aK - 1/h$. This gives the desired increasing returns property without destroying the essential linearity of the production function. Similarly, setting $h < 0$ would allow decreasing returns.

3
Labor-Leisure Choices and the Distribution of Earnings

The parent who leaves his son enormous wealth generally deadens the energies of the son, and tempts him to lead a less useful and less worthy life than he otherwise would.

Andrew Carnegie

The preceding chapter derived the optimal life-cycle consumption plan for a utility-maximizing consumer, contingent upon an assumed —though arbitrary—pattern of earnings. It was observed there that, owing to the assumption of perfect capital markets, only the discounted value of the earnings stream was relevant. More generally, the assumption of a perfect capital market makes the consumption and the labor-supply plans *separable* in a sense to be made more precise shortly. This, in fact, is the motivation for dealing first with the consumption problem in isolation. This chapter takes up the second half of the consumer's optimization problem, his choice of a life-cycle pattern in labor and leisure. It will be seen that the results of Chapter 2 can be derived as part of a more general maximization problem, the maximization of a utility integral that depends upon both consumption and leisure time.

3.1 Choices Open to the Consumer-Worker

As Becker [1965] and others have pointed out, the ultimate constraint upon the consumer is not income nor even wealth, but time. He can allocate his finite economic lifetime among three alternative uses:[1]

1. *Leisure*: Leisure time is assumed to be a direct source of utility. Indeed, if the typical individual has at his disposal 5,864 dis-

1. I ignore here the time taken up by the act of consumption. This, of course, is the essence of the Becker paper just cited.

cretionary hours per year (sixteen hours per day, seven days per week, fifty-two weeks per year), most "full-time" workers take nearly two-thirds of this available time in the form of leisure.

2. *Labor*: Work is assumed *not* to be a source of utility, though doubtless there are many persons who derive satisfaction from performing work. Instead, I assume that people work only to finance consumption. Note that the oft-cited person who "likes his work" is not a refutation of this hypothesis. What would be needed to invalidate the assumption would be a person willing to work voluntarily at a zero wage, that is, who was satiated with leisure. My guess is that there are a few such individuals.

3. *Education*: Somewhere in between the first two uses of time, and sharing some of the characteristics of each, is the third category: education. To some extent, at least for some persons, education is clearly a consumption item, that is, a purchased source of satisfaction. Perhaps more important quantitatively, most forms of education are also investments in human capital, that is, sacrifices of time and money today in order to enhance future earning power.

From the point of view of an optimizing model of household behavior, education has one more very curious property. During most stages of education—college, graduate education, and some forms of on-the-job training being the exceptions—the individual does not choose the training he is to receive. Since most of his education is obtained before he "comes of age," it is his parents (or the state, if school attendance is compulsory) who have the decision-making authority. Only after what I have called "economic age zero," corresponding very roughly to calendar age eighteen, does the typical individual make his own educational decisions. When making these final decisions, the stock of educational capital he "inherits" at, say, age eighteen is an exogenous variable.

These two properties make educational choices by individuals very difficult to model with any pretense of realism. I have been able to obtain some preliminary results with a highly simplified model of educational choices. However, this model is not sufficiently developed to use as a building block in an exact model of income distribution. For these reasons, in the remainder of the book I adopt the drastic polar assumption that there are essentially no educational choices. In particular, the wage rate that an individual can earn at any point in his life is given to him exogenously—as a result of his innate abilities and decisions by his parents—and cannot be influenced. While this notion is qualitatively quite wrong, it is hoped that such errors are not *quantitatively* important. That is, *for purposes of studying income distribution*, the fact that individuals make investments in human capital *as endogenous decisions* may not be terribly important.[2] In any case, the remainder of this chapter is devoted to extending the familiar model of labor-leisure choice by an individual facing a parametric wage into a dynamic context. As such, it may be viewed as complementary to the human-capital model, which deals with dynamic labor-training choices while ignoring leisure. Extension of the present model to incorporate endogenous educational choices is left on the agenda of unfinished business.

Though I speak throughout of an individual worker-consumer, the theoretical model applies equally well to a multi-earner family, so long as the total work burden is distributed optimally within the family. This, of course, is merely a corollary of Samuelson's [1956] theorem on community indifference curves. In the simulation work to follow in Chapters 4 to 6, I restrict myself to single-earner families.

During the individual's working years, the dynamic and static theories are essentially identical. It is only when choice of a retirement period is considered that the dynamics become interesting. The model to follow makes this decision both explicit and endogenous.

3.2 Labor-Leisure Choices over a Finite Lifetime

Consider a household with an instantaneous utility function which is additively separable, $U(C(t)) + V(L(t))$, where C is consumption, L is the fraction of time devoted to leisure, and $U(\cdot)$ and $V(\cdot)$ are utility functions satisfying the usual conditions of positive, but diminishing, marginal utility. Suppose the family is endowed with an initial stock of nonhuman capital K_0 and with skills sufficient to earn a life-cycle pattern of wages $w(t)$ and seeks to maximize lifetime utility. The problem would be to maximize

$$\int_0^T e^{-\rho t}[U(C) + V(L)]\,dt + B[(1-\tau)K_T]$$

2. This, of course, is precisely the opposite point of view from that taken by human-capital theorists such as Becker, Mincer, Chiswick, and others. I have explained in Chapter 1 why I find their models unsatisfactory for present purposes. I hasten to point out that these remarks should *not* be interpreted as a *defense* of the notion that individuals cannot influence their future productivity. Clearly this is fallacious, and the model should be amended to allow at least for educational choices. A notable effort in this direction, though not in the framework of distribution theory, is Weizsäcker [1967]. I only mean to suggest that such modifications are very difficult and may not be of great quantitative import.

subject to a specified K_0 and the constraints

$$C(t) + s(t) = rK(t) + w(t)h(t),$$

$$\dot{K}(t) = s(t),$$

where $h(t) \equiv 1 - L(t)$ is the fraction of time devoted to work.

Substitution of the first constraint into the objective function leads to a typical optimal control problem with one state variable (K) and two control variables $(s$ and $h)$. According to the maximum principle, if the Hamiltonian function is defined as

$$H(K,s,h) = e^{-\rho t}U(rK + wh - s) + e^{-\rho t}V(1-h) + \mu(t)s,$$

first-order conditions for an extremum are[3]

$$\frac{\partial H}{\partial K} = re^{-\rho t}U'(C) = -\dot{\mu}(t); \tag{3.1}$$

$$\frac{\partial H}{\partial s} = -e^{-\rho t}U'(C) + \mu(t) = 0; \tag{3.2}$$

$$\frac{\partial H}{\partial h} = -e^{-\rho t}V'(L) + e^{-\rho t}U'(C)w \leqslant 0, \tag{3.3}$$

with $<$ implying $h = 0$; and the transversality condition

$$\mu(T) = \frac{dB[(1-\tau)K_T]}{dK_T}. \tag{3.4}$$

The reader will notice that the conditions relating to consumption-savings decisions (equations (3.1), (3.2), and (3.4)) are identical to equations (2.4)–(2.6) of Chapter 2. Since these have already been analyzed extensively, I shall simply adapt the results obtained there and concentrate on equation (3.3).

Consider first the working phase where h is positive. Then (3.3) holds as an equality:

$$\frac{V'(L)}{U'(C)} = w(t). \tag{3.5}$$

That is, as in static theory, the consumer equates his marginal rate of substitution between leisure and consumption to the given wage rate.

3. Since $U(\cdot)$, $V(\cdot)$, and $B(\cdot)$ are all assumed to be strictly concave, these conditions are also sufficient for a strong maximum.

The only difference is that $L(t)$, $C(t)$, and $w(t)$ are all liable to be changing over time. Differentiating (3.5) logarithmically yields the following equation of motion for the working phase:

$$\frac{LV''(L)}{V'(L)}\frac{\dot{L}}{L} - \frac{CU''(C)}{U'(C)}\frac{\dot{C}}{C} = \frac{\dot{w}}{w}.$$

Now it was established in Chapter 2 that

$$-\frac{CU''(C)}{U'(C)}\frac{\dot{C}}{C} = r - \rho$$

so that, defining $\epsilon \equiv -LV''(L)/V'(L)$, the preceding expression can be rewritten:

$$\frac{\dot{L}}{L} = \frac{r - \rho - m(t)}{\epsilon} \equiv \gamma(t), \tag{3.6}$$

where $m(t)$ is the instantaneous rate of growth of wages at time t. In the special case where both ϵ and m are constants, equation (3.6) states that leisure grows (or shrinks) at a steady exponential rate γ which is smaller (in absolute value) the larger is ϵ, that is, the faster marginal utility of leisure declines. Equation (3.6) also shows that an individual with relatively low time preference tends to concentrate his work effort in the early years of life, and takes increasing amounts of leisure as he gets older, whereas a worker with very high time preference does the reverse.

Consider next whether there is a "retirement" phase where $h(t) = 0$, and if so, where in the life-cycle it comes. From (3.3), if a corner maximum is reached with $L = 1$, $h = 0$, it must be the case that

$$w(t)U'(C) < V'(1) \equiv \xi. \tag{3.7}$$

When in the life cycle can this occur? The growth rate of the left-hand side of (3.7), which may be interpreted as the utility equivalent of the wage rate, is known to be $\rho - r + m(t)$. Suppose first that $r - m(t)$, which is the rate of discount net of any trend increase in wages, exceeds ρ always. Then the left-hand side of (3.7) is declining steadily as in Figure 3.1a, so that *if* there is a retirement period it would have to come *after* the working phase. This is the sort of life cycle one normally expects. Now consider the opposite case, where $r - m(t)$ is always smaller than ρ. For such an individual the left-hand side of (3.7) would rise steadily, as in Figure 3.1b, so that if there were to be a retirement period, it would have to come *before* the

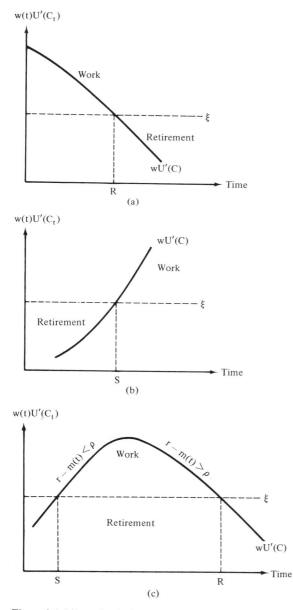

Figure 3.1 Life-cycle choices of work and retirement phases
(a) Work and retirement phases when $r - m(t) > \rho$
(b) Work and retirement phases when $r - m(t) < \rho$
(c) Work and retirement phases when $r - m(t) - \rho$ changes sign

working years.[4] The explanation for this counterintuitive result is
simple. An individual with very high time preference wants to take
his leisure time early in life. This tendency is enhanced if there is an
upward trend in wages, and discouraged by high interest rates, which
make work tomorrow yield little income in present value terms. Of
course, such an individual would borrow heavily to finance consumption in the early stages of his life.

Figure 3.1c depicts what is often taken to be the most realistic
pattern. In the early stages of life $m(t)$ is high so that the left-hand
side of (3.7) rises rapidly. Then, as $m(t)$ falls and finally becomes
negative, the utility equivalent of the wage rate falls. Such a pattern
of wages over the life cycle[5] might induce a person to take two
"retirement" periods, one before work (when wages are too low) and
one after (when wages fall to low again).

The present model can be integrated with the results of Chapter 2,
and some understanding of lifetime work incentives obtained, by
pursuing this analysis further and actually calculating the value of M,
the discounted present value of lifetime earnings. Under perfect
capital markets, this is the only aspect of the labor-leisure plan which
is relevant to the consumption-bequest plan. The question to be
investigated is, How do lifetime earnings depend on wages, inheritance and tastes? This is obviously a question of some importance for
the income distribution. To answer this, I need specific functional
forms for the utility functions and a specific time path for $m(t)$. For
the latter I shall assume $m(t) = m$, that is, a constant rate of growth of
wages. In fact there are two distinct factors operating on the wage at
time t of a vintage v man, $w_v(t)$. First, there is a typical age-wage
pattern for any given vintage which may be rising at first and then
falling. Second, there is the background rate of growth of real wages
in the economy. To characterize the sum of these two influences as
steady exponential growth at a rate m does not seem to do a grave
injustice to the truth.[6]

As has been noted above, when r, ρ, and m are all constant there
can be (at most) one retirement period—either at the start or end of

4. In the special case where $r - m(t) = \rho$, the left-hand side is constant. If this were true
for the entire life cycle, the individual would either always be at work or never work at
all.
5. The usual human-capital explanation for this age-wage profile holds that younger
workers are investing heavily in nonschool human capital, thus raising their future
productivity, while mature workers invest much less. An alternative explanation, with
the same observable consequences, is simply that experience raises productivity but is
subject to diminishing returns.
6. For more on this, see Section 4.2 below.

life. So for any individual, *given the initial conditions* L_0 and C_0, equations (3.6) and (3.7) trace out the complete life cycle in labor and leisure. However, finding these initial conditions and, in particular, showing how they depend on endowments and tastes, is not an easy task. Section 3.3 below is devoted to this undertaking. The analysis is quite technical, and some readers may not be interested in the details; so in the remainder of this section I "borrow" some results of Section 3.3 to show what light they shed on lifetime work incentives in a very simple case.

In particular, suppose that $r - m > \rho$, and take the elasticities of marginal utility of both consumption and leisure to be unity, that is, adopt the Cobb-Douglas form for the instantaneous utility function: $\log(C) + \xi \log(L)$. For such a utility function, equation (3.5) at time zero implies[7]

$$L_0 = \frac{\xi}{w_0} C_0. \tag{3.8}$$

Suppose there is no retirement, that is, in Figure 3.1a $w(T)U'(C_T) > \xi$. Since the time profile of labor supply is $h(t) = 1 - e^{\gamma t}L_0$, the discounted value of lifetime earnings is

$$M = \int_0^T w_0 e^{mt}(1 - L_0 e^{\gamma t})e^{-rt}\,dt$$

or

$$M = w_0[N(r - m, T) - L_0 N(\rho, T)],$$

where I have again employed the notation

$$N(a,T) \equiv \int_0^T e^{-at}\,dt,$$

and have used the fact that $\gamma - r + m = -\rho$ when $\epsilon = 1$. It follows that the marginal reduction in earnings per dollar of inherited wealth is

$$\frac{\partial M}{\partial K_0} = -w_0 N(\rho, T)\frac{\partial L_0}{\partial K_0} = -\xi N(\rho, T)\frac{\partial C_0}{\partial K_0} \qquad \text{by (3.8)}.$$

7. Recall that the first part of life must be the working phase if there is any working phase at all.

Now, from equation (2.14')

$$\frac{\partial C_0}{\partial K_0} = \frac{1}{N(\rho, T) + b} \left[1 + \frac{\partial M}{\partial K_0} \right].$$

Solving these two equations simultaneously gives the desired disincentive effect as

$$\frac{\partial M}{\partial K_0} = - \frac{\xi N(\rho, T)}{(1 + \xi) N(\rho, T) + b},$$

(3.9)

which is negative but larger than -1 as might be expected.

Equation (3.9) has a straightforward intuitive interpretation. First, suppose there were no bequest motive so that $b = 0$. In that case (3.9) reduces to $\partial M / \partial K_0 = -\xi/(1+\xi)$. That is, for every dollar of inherited wealth, the family reduces its lifetime earned income by a fraction that increases with the relative weight attached to leisure in its utility function. Note that the size of the disincentive effect depends *only* on tastes (and the length of life, if $b > 0$) and *not* on the level of K_0 nor on the wage. These properties are inherent in the Cobb-Douglas specification. If the utility function were in the canonical Cobb-Douglas form, with weights summing to unity, the weight for leisure would be $\xi/(1 + \xi)$. It is well known that such a consumer chooses to "spend" a fraction $\xi/(1 + \xi)$ of his real income (measured in monetary units) in the form of leisure (where leisure time is valued at the wage rate), and that this fraction is independent of scale. This, of course, is the result just obtained. If ξ is extremely high, there is an almost dollar-for-dollar reduction in income when an inheritance (or a government welfare check) is received; conversely, if ξ is low, disincentive effects are minimal.

By now it should be clear to the reader that the distribution of ξ across the population is crucial to the income distribution. If inheritors of large fortunes have high ξ's (that is, value leisure highly), while poor people have low ξ's, earnings tend to mitigate the inequalities caused by inheritance. By contrast, if the "psychology of poverty" makes poor people leisure-lovers and "middle-class values" make those in higher economic strata consumption-lovers, there is no tendency toward equalization; on the contrary, earnings patterns tend to replicate inheritance patterns. A variety of assumptions about the distribution of ξ across the population will be *quantitatively* explored in the next chapter.

The bequest motive ($b > 0$) has the obvious effect of lessening work disincentives since it provides an additional use for earned income (other than consumption). Low values of b, of course, have little impact so the statements above are approximately true. More precisely, the elasticity of $\partial M / \partial K_0$ with respect to b, which is always less than unity in any case, approaches zero as b approaches zero.

3.3 Analytical Solutions: The Problem of Initial Conditions

The *qualitative* features of the consumer's life cycle have been adequately described in Chapter 2 (where consumption-savings decisions are concerned) and Section 3.2 above (where labor-leisure decisions are concerned); most of these features apply equally well to more general utility functions. However, if one desires to simulate an economy composed of a number of such individuals, one must sacrifice generality in order to analyze the *quantitative* aspects of the life-cycle under specific functional forms. For example, it is necessary to know precisely how much an individual with given tastes, inheritance and wage rate actually earns over his lifetime. The computations involved are often quite cumbersome, and the treatment to follow is regrettably taxonomic.

As a preliminary step, before proceeding to the individual cases, it will be helpful to collect those results already established which hold in every possible instance. First, if S denotes the age of starting work and R denotes the age of retirement,[8] the general expression for lifetime earnings is

$$M = \int_S^R w_0 e^{-(r-m)t}(1 - L(t))\, dt. \tag{3.10}$$

It was established in Chapter 2 that $C(t) = C_0 e^{gt}$ and in this chapter that

$$L(t) = L(S)e^{\gamma t} \tag{3.11}$$

whenever $L < 1$. Also derived in Chapter 2 were two implicit relations between initial consumption and the optimal bequest, repeated here for the reader's convenience:

(2.10) $K_T e^{-rT} + C_0 N(r - g, T) = K_0 + M,$

(2.13) $K_T = b(1 - \tau)^{(1-\beta)/\beta} e^{(rT)/\beta} C_0^{\delta/\beta}.$

Substituting (2.13) into (2.10) gives an expression for the sum of the

8. I have established above that $S = 0$ or $R = T$, or both.

discounted present values of consumption and bequests in terms of C_0 alone:

$$f(C_0) \equiv N(r-g,T)C_0 + BC_0^{\delta/\beta} = K_0 + M, \tag{3.12}$$

where $B \equiv b[(1-\tau)e^{-rT}]^{(1-\beta)/\beta}.$

3.3.1 The Case where $\gamma = 0$ $(r - m = \rho)$

I shall introduce the techniques to be used by starting with the simplest and least interesting possibility, namely the knife-edge case where $\gamma = 0$, that is, where $r - m = \rho$.[9] There are only two possible outcomes: either the entire life is spent working at some constant rate ($S = 0$, $R = T$, $L = L_0$) or the entire life is spent at leisure ($S = T$, $R = 0$, $L = 1$).

If any work is performed, equation (3.5) must hold at time zero. With the specific functional forms adopted, this can be solved for the (constant) amount of leisure:

$$L_0 = \left(\frac{\xi C_0^{\delta}}{w_0} \right)^{1/\epsilon}. \tag{3.13}$$

Using this formula in equation (3.10) with $S = 0$ and $R = T$ gives

$$M = w_0 N(r-m,T)(1-L_0).$$

Finally, substituting this into (3.12) gives the basic implicit equation for C_0,

$$f(C_0) = K_0 + w_0 N(r-m,T)(1-L_0)$$

or, in abbreviated notation,

$$f(C_0) = K_0 + w_0 h(C_0), \tag{3.14}$$

where

$$h(C_0) \equiv N(r-m,T)(1-L_0) \tag{3.15}$$

gives lifetime discounted earnings, deflated by w_0.

The solution of this nonlinear equation in C_0 is depicted in Figure

9. If ρ has a continuous probability distribution over the population, this case occurs on a set of measure zero.

3.2. Straightforward computations show that

$$f(0)=0, \qquad h(0)=w_0 N(r-m,T)>0,$$
$$f'(C_0)>0, \qquad h'(C_0)<0.$$

There is also a natural limit on the range of C_0 since L_0 cannot be greater than unity. Let $\hat{C}$ denote this maximal value of C_0, obtained by setting $L_0=1$ in (3.13):

$$\hat{C}=\left(\frac{w_0}{\xi}\right)^{1/\delta}. \tag{3.16}$$

Since $h(\hat{C})=0$, given K_0 the value of $\hat{C}$ can be read from Figure 3.2 as shown. There are two possibilities. For low and moderate values of K_0 (such as K_0^b), $\hat{C}$ is some high level such as $\hat{C}_b$. The solution is then at C_0^*, and leisure begins at some level less than 100%, as determined by (3.13). However, if K_0 is sufficiently high (see K_0^a in Figure 3.2), the constraint $L_0 \leqslant 1$ is binding, so that the solution is at $\hat{C}_a$ with no work performed. Stated succinctly:

Proposition 3.1 For an individual whose rate of subjective time discounting equals $r-m$,
1. if $K_0 \geqslant f(\hat{C})$, he will never work;
2. if $K_0 < f(\hat{C})$, he will never retire.

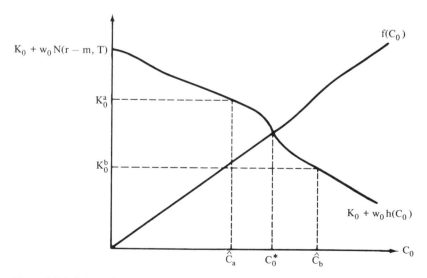

Figure 3.2 Solution of equation (3.14) for optimal initial consumption

In other words, an inheritance large enough to finance the consumption and bequest plan implicit in $C_0 = \hat{C}$ induces complete withdrawal from the labor force, while a less generous inheritance leads the recipient to spend his entire life at work. Of course, this shows that noninheritors always work at any positive wage, and that "every person has his price" in the sense that for each individual there is an inheritance large enough to lead him to pursue a life of leisure. Hereafter I shall refer to the plan implicitly defined by $C_0 = \hat{C}$ as "opulence." Note the determinants of $\hat{C}$ in (3.16). When wages are high and the taste for leisure is low, $\hat{C}$ is high, and a life of work is likely. Conversely, low wages and a high taste for leisure produces a low standard of "opulence" and thus makes a life at leisure more probable.

3.3.2 The Case where $\gamma > 0$ $(r - m > \rho)$

When the difference between the rate of interest and the rate of growth of real wages exceeds the rate of time discounting, the fraction of time devoted to work falls over the working life. Since the wage converted into utility units, $w(t)U'(C)$, falls steadily as in Figure 3.1a, there are three possibilities to be considered:
1. There is no retirement $(R = T)$. This occurs if $w(0)U'(C_0)$ is very high and or declines very slowly so that $w(T)U'(C_T) > \xi$ in Figure 3.1a.
2. There is no work $(R = 0)$. This occurs if $w(0)U'(C_0) < \xi$.
3. There is an initial phase of work followed by a final phase of retirement $(0 < R < T)$. This case obtains if $w(T)U'(C_T) < \xi < w(0)U'(C_0)$.

Now in each of these cases, $L(t) = L_0 e^{\gamma t}$ so (3.10) may be written

$$M = w_0[N(r - m, R) - L_0 N(r - m - \gamma, R)]. \tag{3.17}$$

Since at $t = 0$ some positive amount of work is performed (except in the trivial case where $R = 0$), equation (3.5) holds,

$$\xi C_0^\delta = w_0 L_0^\epsilon. \tag{3.18}$$

Finally (see Figure 3.1a), the retirement age R is defined implicitly by $w(R)U'(C(R)) = \xi$, or

$$w_0 e^{mR} = \xi C(R)^\delta = \xi C_0^\delta e^{(r - \rho)R}.$$

This last expression, (3.17), and (3.18) are three equations which implicitly define M, L_0, and C_0 as functions of R.

Substitution of these functions into the lifetime budget restraint, equation (3.12), results in a single implicit equation for R:

$$N(r - g, T)\hat{C}e^{-[(r-m-\rho)/\delta]R} + B\hat{C}^{\delta/\beta}e^{-[(r-m-\rho)/\beta]R}$$

$$= K_0 + w_0[N(r-m,R) - e^{-\gamma R}N(r-m-\gamma,R)], \qquad (3.19)$$

where I have used the definition that $L(R) = L_0e^{\gamma R} = 1$ to replace L_0 by $e^{-\gamma R}$. Now adopt the following abbreviated notation:

$$F(R) \equiv N(r-g,T)\hat{C}e^{-[(r-m-\rho)/\delta]R} + B\hat{C}^{\delta/\beta}e^{-[(r-m-\rho)/\beta]R} \qquad (3.20)$$

$$H(R) \equiv N(r-m,R) - e^{-\gamma R}N(r-m-\gamma,R), \qquad (3.21)$$

so that $F(R)$ gives total lifetime expenditures and $H(R)$ gives lifetime earnings deflated by w_0, each expressed as a function of R, the retirement age. Note that

$$F(R) = f\left[\hat{C}e^{-[(r-m-\rho)/\delta]R}\right],$$

that is, the present value of the consumption-bequest plan defined by

$$C_0 = \hat{C}e^{-[(r-m-\rho)/\delta]R}.$$

In this shorthand, equation (3.19) becomes

$$F(R) = K_0 + w_0H(R). \qquad (3.22)$$

Clearly there is no general analytical solution to (3.22), but it is easy to prove that a unique solution for R (possibly $R=0$) always exists. The solution is depicted in Figure 3.3. As the reader may readily verify from (3.20) and (3.21), in the present case ($\gamma > 0$)

$$F(0) = f(\hat{C}) > 0, \qquad\qquad H(0) = 0,$$
$$F'(R) < 0, \qquad\qquad\qquad H'(R) > 0,$$
$$F(T) = f\left[\hat{C}e^{-[(r-m-\rho)/\delta]T}\right] > 0 \qquad H(T) > 0.$$

There are, of course, two constraints that do not appear in Figure 3.3. An individual cannot retire before economic age zero; nor may his retirement age exceed T, his age at death. The reader may verify the following proposition by referring to Figure 3.3.

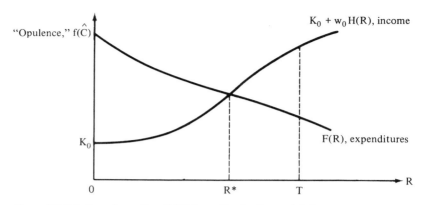

Figure 3.3 Solution of equation (3.22) for optimal retirement date

Proposition 3.2 For an individual whose rate of subjective time discounting is less than $r - m$:

1. if $K_0 \geqslant f(\hat{C})$,   he will choose no working phase ($R = 0$);

2. if $K_0 \leqslant F(T) - w_0 H(T)$,   he will choose no retirement period ($R = T$);

3. if $f(\hat{C}) > K_0 > F(T) - w_0 H(T)$,   he will select an endogenous retirement age according to equation (3.22).

In plain English, if inherited wealth is sufficient to finance the opulent expenditure plan, then no work effort is performed; if inherited wealth is so low that even an entire life at work will not finance the less generous consumption plan defined by $C_0 = \hat{C}^{-[(r-m-\rho)/\delta]T} < \hat{C}$, then the person foregoes retirement entirely; if the inheritance falls anywhere between these extremes the individual retires during some period at the end of his life cycle.[10]

Proposition 3.2 provides a constructive technique for computing the optimal R for each individual. In the simulations reported in later chapters, (3.22) was solved numerically by Newton's method and convergence was quite rapid.

3.3.3 The Case where $\gamma < 0$ ($r - m < \rho$)

It remains to consider those individuals whose rates of subjective time discounting exceed $r - m$. It has already been established that *if*

10. The reader will notice that as $\gamma \to 0$, $F(T) \to F(0) \to f(\hat{C})$ and $H(T) \to 0$, so that Proposition 3.2 reduces to Proposition 3.1.

such a person chooses to take any retirement, he takes it at the start of his life cycle. So there are again three possibilities:
1. There is no retirement ($S=0$). In Figure 3.1b, this is a person for whom $w(0)U'(C_0)>\xi$.
2. There is no work ($S=T$). In Figure 3.1b, this is a person for whom $w(T)U'(C_T)<\xi$.
3. There is an initial retirement phase, from age 0 until age S, followed by a working period from age S to age T ($0<S<T$). Persons of this variety have $w(0)U'(C_0)<\xi<w(T)U'(C_T)$ as depicted in Figure 3.1b.
    To analyze this case, suppose the last possibility prevails. Then leisure time falls over the period $[S,T]$, that is, $L(t)=L_Se^{\gamma(t-S)}=e^{\gamma(t-S)}$, since at the transitional date $L_S=1$. Substituting this path for hours of leisure into (3.10) gives

$$M = w_0e^{-(r-m)S}[N(r-m,T-S)-N(r-m-\gamma,T-S)]. \qquad (3.23)$$

Reference to Figure 3.1b shows that the age of starting work is implicitly defined by $U'(C_S)w(S)=\xi$, or, in the particular case now being scrutinized,

$$C_0=(w_0/\xi)^{1/\delta}e^{-[(r-m-\rho)/\delta]S}=\hat{C}e^{-[(r-m-\rho)/\delta]S}. \qquad (3.24)$$

Substitution of (3.23) and (3.24) into (3.12) gives the basic implicit equation for S:

$$N(r-g,T)\hat{C}e^{-[(r-\rho-m)/\delta]S}+B\hat{C}^{\delta/\beta}e^{-[(r-\rho-m)/\beta]S}$$

$$= K_0+w_0e^{-(r-m)S}[N(r-m,T-S)-N(r-m-\gamma,T-S)]. \qquad (3.25)$$

With the abbreviated notation

$$\hat{H}(S)\equiv e^{-(r-m)S}[N(r-m,T-S)-N(r-m-\gamma,T-S)], \qquad (3.26)$$

equation (3.25) can be rewritten as

$$F(S)=K_0+w_0\hat{H}(S) \qquad (3.27)$$

where $F(\cdot)$ is the same function defined in equation (3.20).
    Once again, although an analytical solution for S is impossible, it is easy to establish that *if a solution exists*, it is unique. Simply notice

that since in the present case $r - m - \rho < 0$:

$$F(0) = f(\hat{C}) > 0, \qquad \hat{H}(0) > 0,$$
$$F'(S) > 0, \qquad\qquad \hat{H}'(S) < 0,$$
$$F(T) > 0, \qquad\qquad \hat{H}(T) = 0.$$

Figure 3.4 depicts the solution of equation (3.27). As before there are two implicit constraints upon the choice of S; namely that $S \geqslant 0$ and $S \leqslant T$. The nature of the solution is outlined by

Proposition 3.3 For an individual whose subjective rate of time discounting is greater than $r - m$,

1. if $K_0 \leqslant F(0) - w_0\hat{H}(0)$,   he will work his entire life ($S = 0$);

2. if $K_0 \geqslant F(T)$,   he will choose to spend his entire life in retirement ($S = T$);

3. if $F(T) > K_0 > F(0) - w_0\hat{H}(0)$,   he will select an interior work-starting age S, as defined by (3.27), spending the first S years of his life in retirement and the last $T - S$ at work ($0 < S < T$).

Intuitively, if the consumer cannot finance the opulent consumption-bequest plan even by working his entire life, he foregoes idleness

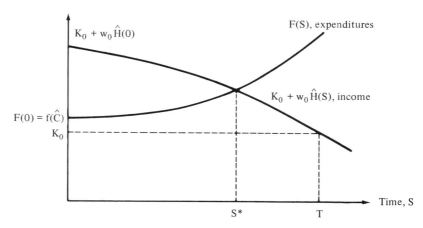

Figure 3.4 Solution of equation (3.27) for optimal work-starting date

entirely; if his inheritance alone is sufficient to support the "super opulent" plan defined by $C_0 = \hat{C}e^{-[(r-m-\rho)/\delta]T} > \hat{C}$, he never begins working; and if his inheritance is between these limits, he spends the early part of his life in retirement and works the remainder.[11]

Comparing this to the previous proposition reveals a certain asymmetry. For persons who retire late in life, inherited wealth had only to exceed $F(0) = f(\hat{C})$ to lead to a life of idleness. By contrast, in the present case inherited wealth must exceed some larger amount, $F(T)$. Further, in the present case a person will be persuaded to forego retirement entirely as long as $f(\hat{C})$ exceeds total income from a full life of work. The corresponding condition for persons who retire late in life is that $F(T)$ (which for these people is smaller than $f(\hat{C})$) exceed income from a full life's work. In other words, people with $r - m > \rho$ seem more prone to take retirement periods than people with $r - m < \rho$. Why should this be so? The answer is that persons with very high time preference prefer to concentrate whatever labor they perform in the later years of life. But work performed very late in life contributes little to lifetime *discounted* earnings. Thus, if effort is postponed, a greater amount of labor is required to produce the same lifetime discounted earnings. Since hours of leisure decline exponentially with time, this necessitates a shorter retirement period.

As before, Proposition 3.3 provides a constructive technique for finding the optimal date of starting work, and thus the entire optimal leisure-consumption-bequest plan, for an individual with arbitrary tastes and endowments. Newton's method again proved to be an efficient algorithm for computing numerical solutions.

3.4 Comparative Dynamics of the Labor-Leisure Plan

Having developed the implicit equations that define the optimal plan for every consumer, it is worth investigating how the solution depends on the various parameters. Of particular interest are the responses of labor supply and earnings to those parameters that the government can influence directly; namely, K_0 (through lump-sum transfers), w_0 (through the income tax), and τ (the inheritance tax rate). For purposes of such comparative-dynamic exercises, there are

---

11. Again, note that as $r - m - \rho \to 0$, $F(T) \to F(0) \to f(\hat{C})$, and $\hat{H}(0) \to 0$, so Proposition 3.3 reduces to Proposition 3.1.

essentially four distinct cases:
1. Persons who elect to take no retirement ($S=0$ or $R=T$).
2. Persons who elect to do no work ($S=T$ or $R=0$).
3. Persons who elect to take a retirement period late in life ($0<R<T$).
4. Persons who elect to take a retirement period at the start of the life cycle ($0<S<T$).

The remainder of this section treats each of these cases in turn, investigating the effects on lifetime labor supply, earnings, and retirement period (if any) of changes in the key parameters. Once again, the reader not interested in the details may safely skim this section.

An important preliminary question is, How should *lifetime labor supply* be measured? Since work effort is spread over the life cycle, this is a problem in intertemporal aggregation. An obvious measure would appear to be M/w_0, that is, lifetime discounted earnings normalized by the wage level at time zero. In fact, this measure has more than just simplicity to recommend it. Observe that changes in the parameters (other than r and m) do not change the *relative* present-value prices of labor at any two points in time: $w(t_1)/w(t_2) = e^{-(r-m)(t_1-t_2)}$. Thus, taking a cue from the Hicks [1946] composite goods theorem, it is natural to define a composite commodity (called "lifetime labor supply") by weighting labor supply at each moment by its relative price. This composite commodity would be

$$H \equiv \int_0^T h(t)e^{-(r-m)t}\,dt.$$

It can be shown that the supply of lifetime labor thus defined obeys the usual Hicks-Slutsky conditions; that is, the supply of H may be normal or "backward bending," but the *compensated* supply curve must be upward sloping.[12] As the reader may have discerned, it turns out that M/w_0, the "obvious" measure, is equal to H, the Hicksian composite good. I therefore adopt H as the measure of lifetime work effort to be used throughout.

3.4.1 Life Cycles with No Retirement
Regardless of the sign of γ, when the entire lifetime is spent at work the time path of leisure is given by

$$L(t) = L_0 e^{\gamma t}$$

12. On the Slutsky equation for this problem, see Appendix 3.1.

where

$$0 < L_0 = \left(\frac{\xi C_0^{\delta}}{w_0}\right)^{1/\epsilon} < 1.$$

Substituting this, along with $S = 0$ and $R = T$, into (3.10), and the resulting expression for earnings into (3.12), results in the basic equation for initial consumption:

$$f(C_0)$$
$$= K_0 + w_0 \left[N(r - m, T) - (\xi/w_0)^{1/\epsilon} C_0^{\delta/\epsilon} N(r - m - \gamma, T) \right], \quad (3.28)$$

where $f(\cdot)$ is as defined in (3.12). This equation contains all the comparative-dynamic information of the model. Defining

$$h(C_0) \equiv N(r - m, T) - (\xi/w_0)^{1/\epsilon} C_0^{\delta/\epsilon} N(r - m - \gamma, T) \quad (3.29)$$

makes it possible to write (3.28) more compactly as

$$f(C_0) = K_0 + w_0 h(C_0) \quad (3.30)$$

which brings out the strong analogies with equations (3.14), (3.22), and (3.27).

Consider first the lifetime labor supply. The reader will probably have noticed by now that in the present case $H = h(C_0)$ with $h'(C_0) < 0$, so the problem boils down to analyzing the behavior of C_0 in (3.30). Applying the implicit function theorem to (3.30) yields

$$\frac{dC_0}{dK_0} = \frac{1}{f'(C_0) - w_0 h'(C_0)} > 0, \quad (3.31)$$

$$\frac{dC_0}{dw_0} = \frac{h(C_0) + w_0 \left[(1/\epsilon)(\xi/w_0)^{1/\epsilon}(1/w_0) C_0^{\delta/\epsilon} N(r - m - \gamma, T)\right]}{f'(C_0) - w_0 h'(C_0)} > 0,$$

$$(3.32)$$

$$\frac{dC_0}{d\tau} = \frac{(\partial B/\partial \tau) C_0^{\delta/\beta}}{f'(C_0) - w_0 h'(C_0)} = \frac{1 - \beta}{\beta} \frac{C_0^{\delta/\beta} B/(1 - \tau)}{f'(C_0) - w_0 h'(C_0)}. \quad (3.33)$$

The last expression has the same sign as $1 - \beta$. That is, if the marginal utility of bequests declines faster than the logarithmic case

($\beta > 1$), the expression is negative so that higher inheritance taxes stifle consumption; and if marginal utility declines more slowly than this, the expression is positive so that higher inheritance taxes induce more consumption.

From (3.31), the effect of inherited wealth, or any other lump-sum grant, on lifetime work effort is

$$\frac{dH}{dK_0} = \frac{h'(C_0)}{f'(C_0) - w_0 h'(C_0)} \tag{3.34}$$

which is unambiguously negative, the usual income effect on labor supply. Since the denominator is the lifetime marginal propensity to consume (as shown by (3.31)), this establishes the intuitively appealing result that individuals with high propensities to consume have small disincentive effects, and vice versa. And this finding holds under the assumption that the consumption and leisure components of utility are strongly separable, that is, the marginal rate of substitution between leisure in any two periods is independent of the pattern of consumption. Allowing positive interactions between leisure and consumption (for example, one enjoys leisure time by purchasing consumption goods and services) can only strengthen this conclusion.

I noted early in this chapter that the way in which lifetime earnings $M = w_0 H$ react to inherited wealth is of particular importance for the income distribution. By (3.34) the relevant derivative is

$$\frac{dM}{dK_0} = w_0 \frac{dH}{dK_0} = \frac{w_0 h'(C_0)}{f'(C_0) - w_0 h'(C_0)},$$

which is negative but greater than -1 *for all persons regardless of tastes*. That is, a person receiving a lump-sum gift of one dollar will never fail to reduce his own earnings in response; but he will not reduce his earnings by as much as the original dollar.

Consider next the effect on labor supply and earnings of changes in the wage rate. Since $H = h(C_0)$,

$$\frac{dH}{dw_0} = h'(C_0) \frac{dC_0}{dw_0} + \frac{\partial h}{\partial w_0}\bigg|_{C_0 = \text{const.}}, \tag{3.35}$$

which is the usual result that the effect of the wage on the supply of work effort is theoretically ambiguous. The first term is always negative by (3.32), but the second term is always positive. As in static theory, however, it is possible to break up the total effect of the wage on labor supply into income and substitution effects. In particular, according to Slutsky's decomposition:

$$\frac{dH}{dw_0}\bigg|_{K_0=\text{const.}} = \frac{dH}{dw_0}\bigg|_{\text{utility}=\text{const.}} + H\frac{dH}{dK_0}. \tag{3.36}$$

From (3.31) and (3.35),

$$\frac{dH}{dw_0}\bigg|_{K_0=\text{const.}} = \frac{\partial h}{\partial w_0} + \frac{h'(C_0)h(C_0) + w_0 h'(C_0)(\partial h/\partial w_0)}{f'(C_0) - w_0 h'(C_0)}.$$

And from the Slutsky equation and (3.34),

$$\frac{dH}{dw_0}\bigg|_{K_0=\text{const.}} = \frac{dH}{dw_0}\bigg|_{U=\text{const.}} + \frac{h'(C_0)h(C_0)}{f'(C_0) - w_0 h'(C_0)}.$$

Equating these two expressions gives the following formula for the compensated substitution effect:

$$\frac{dH}{dw_0}\bigg|_{U=\text{const.}} = \frac{\partial h}{\partial w_0}\left[1 + \frac{w_0 h'}{f' - w_0 h'}\right] = \frac{\partial h}{\partial w_0}\left[1 + \frac{\partial M}{\partial K_0}\right],$$

which is unambiguously positive by a previous result. This line of reasoning, incidentally, points out that it is the logic of maximizing behavior—as summarized in the Slutsky term—that makes it impossible for an individual to reduce M more than dollar-for-dollar in response to a lump-sum gift.

Work effort may rise or fall when the wage level rises; however, it is easily established that earnings must rise. In particular,

$$\frac{dM}{dw_0} = H + w_0 \frac{dH}{dw_0}.$$

Substitution of (3.35) into this leads, after a little manipulation, to

$$\frac{dM}{dw_0} = \left[H + w_0 \frac{\partial h}{\partial w_0}\right]\left[1 + \frac{\partial M}{\partial K_0}\right] > 0.$$

So the same logic of maximizing behavior that ruled out "irrational" responses to lump-sum grants also rules out "irrational" responses to increases in wages.

The remaining parameter of interest here is the inheritance tax rate τ. By (3.33) $dH/d\tau$ has the sign of $\beta - 1$. That is, if β exceeds unity estate taxation is work-inducing, while if β falls short of unity raising τ provides a work disincentive. In the logarithmic case ($\beta = 1$), inheritance taxation continues to have no distorting effects.

3.4.2 Life Cycles with No Work

Cases for which the optimum plan includes no work are trivial to analyze. The wage rate can, of course, have no effect on behavior (unless it pushes the individual across the borderline and induces him to start working); when $H = 0$ the compensated and uncompensated effects of w_0 are both the same and are zero. From (3.12) with $M = 0$ the impact of lump-sum income on initial consumption is

$$\frac{dC_0}{dK_0} = \frac{1}{N(r-g,T) + (B\delta/\beta)C_0^{\delta/\beta-1}} .$$

If there is no bequest motive ($B = 0$), this is constant and the lifetime marginal propensity to consume (MPC) is always equal to unity.[13] The bequest motive makes the lifetime MPC smaller than one and rising, constant, or falling according as $\delta < \beta$, $\delta = \beta$, or $\delta > \beta$. As in the case of no retirement, the effect of τ on C_0 has the sign of $1 - \beta$, and is smaller (in absolute value) the larger is the lifetime MPC.

3.4.3 Life Cycles with Late Retirement

For individuals who select an unconstrained retirement age $R < T$, there is a new wrinkle in the comparative dynamics of the model: changes in parameters may—and generally will—lead to changes in the optimal retirement age.

Assuming the individual reaches an interior maximum both before and after the change in parameters, total differentiation of (3.22) yields

$$F'(R)dR + \frac{\partial F}{\partial w_0}dw_0 + \frac{\partial F}{\partial \tau}d\tau = dK_0 + H(R)dw_0 + w_0 H'(R)dR.$$

The partial effects of w_0, K_0, and τ on R follow immediately:

$$\frac{\partial R}{\partial K_0} = \frac{1}{F'(R) - w_0 H'(R)} < 0, \tag{3.37}$$

$$\frac{\partial R}{\partial w_0} = \frac{H(R) - \partial F/\partial w_0}{F'(R) - w_0 H'(R)}, \tag{3.38}$$

$$\frac{\partial R}{\partial \tau} = \frac{-\partial F/\partial \tau}{F'(R) - w_0 H'(R)} . \tag{3.39}$$

13. Because lifetime consumption, in present value terms, is $C_0 N(r-g,T)$.

As expected, greater inherited wealth lengthens the retirement period, but the two prices (w_0 and τ) have ambiguous effects.

The impact of each parameter on lifetime labor supply follows immediately from (3.37)–(3.39) by multiplying each expression by $H'(R) > 0$. Of course, inherited wealth lowers work effort while wages and inheritance taxes may have either effect. Since $M = w_0 H$, the impact of lump-sum income on lifetime earnings can be obtained simply by multiplying (3.37) by $w_0 H'(R)$. Thus,

$$\frac{\partial M}{\partial K_0} = \frac{w_0 H'(R)}{F'(R) - w_0 H'(R)},$$

which again is negative but greater than -1.

The wage rate has an indeterminate effect on labor supply:

$$\frac{\partial H}{\partial w_0} = \frac{H'(R)[H(R) - \partial F / \partial w_0]}{F'(R) - w_0 H'(R)}.$$

But, of course, the Slutsky term has no such ambiguity:

$$\left. \frac{dH}{dw_0} \right|_{U = \text{const.}} = \left. \frac{dH}{dw_0} \right|_{K_0 = \text{const.}} - H \left. \frac{dH}{dK_0} \right|_{w_0 = \text{const.}}$$

$$= \frac{H'(R)[H(R) - \partial F / \partial w_0]}{F'(R) - w_0 H'(R)} - H \frac{H'(R)}{F'(R) - w_0 H'(R)}$$

$$= \frac{-H'(R) \partial F / \partial w_0}{F'(R) - w_0 H'(R)} > 0.$$

As before, it is a simple matter to prove that although labor supply may respond in either direction to an increase in the wage, earnings must increase.

3.4.4 Life Cycles with Early Retirement

This case can be treated briefly in the same manner as the case just considered. As long as the individual continues to select an interior work-starting date S, the crucial relation is (3.27). Its total differential is

$$F'(S)dS + \frac{\partial F}{\partial w_0} dw_0 + \frac{\partial F}{\partial \tau} d\tau = dK_0 + w_0 \hat{H}'(S)dS + \hat{H}dw_0.$$

The impacts of the parameters on the length of the retirement period follow immediately:

$$\frac{\partial S}{\partial K_0} = \frac{1}{F'(S) - w_0 \hat{H}'(S)} > 0;$$

$$\frac{\partial S}{\partial w_0} = \frac{\hat{H}(S) - \partial F/\partial w_0}{F'(S) - w_0 \hat{H}'(S)}, \qquad \text{which is ambiguous;}$$

$$\frac{\partial S}{\partial \tau} = \frac{-\partial F/\partial \tau}{F'(S) - w_0 \hat{H}'(S)}, \qquad \text{which is ambiguous.}$$

Effects on work effort follow from these by multiplying by $\hat{H}'(S) < 0$, and effects on earnings follow in the obvious way. The results which can be obtained are the same:

1. Lump-sum income has a disincentive effect on work.
2. But this disincentive is never strong enough to offset the gain in lifetime income.
3. Increases in the wage rate have an ambiguous effect on labor supply, but always serve to raise earnings.
4. The compensated substitution effect of w_0 on H is positive.
5. An increase in the inheritance tax rate tends to shorten the retirement period (and increase labor supply and earnings) if β exceeds unity; it has the reverse effects if β is less than unity.

Appendix 3.1 On Deriving the Slutsky Equation

Several times in Section 3.4 reference was made to a "Slutsky equation" for lifetime labor supply, namely

$$(3.36) \qquad \left. \frac{dH}{dw_0} \right|_{U=\text{const.}} = \left. \frac{dH}{dw_0} \right|_{K_0=\text{const.}} - H \frac{dH}{dK_0}.$$

I identified, without proof, the left-hand side of this equation as the compensated substitution effect, that is, the effect of the wage on H, given a constant level of lifetime utility.

To prove that this is actually the Slutsky term it is necessary to show that the amount of lump-sum income K_0 which must be taken away to compensate for the rise in the wage so that the individual remains at the same utility level is

$$\left. \frac{\partial K_0}{\partial w_0} \right|_{U=\text{const.}} = -H. \qquad (3.40)$$

It has been suggested to me that this follows as a direct application of the Hicks composite-commodity theorem since $e^{-(r-m)t}$ are the (unchanged) relative prices of the basic commodities $h(t)$, and therefore the composite commodity

$$H = \int_0^T h(t) e^{-(r-m)t} dt$$

behaves as if it were itself a basic commodity. While this argument is persuasive, and its conclusion correct, it remains the case that Hicks-Slutsky theory—including the composite-commodity theorem—has been proven only for the case of a finite number of commodities. Here I am dealing with a continuum of commodities and, as the general equilibrium theorists have taught us, properties which are easy to establish for a finite commodity space are often terribly difficult to extend into an infinite-dimensional space.

It is not my intention to prove that the entire Hicks-Slutsky theory of demand can be extended to a continuum of commodities, nor even that the composite commodity theorem can be so extended. The sole purpose of this appendix is to prove that equation (3.36), which I offer as a "Slutsky equation," is in fact a valid expression for the compensated labor supply function. As just stated, this amounts to proving equation (3.40).

Indifference curves in infinite-dimensional spaces are quite complicated things. To be able to write them down, I shall have to lean very heavily on the convenient functional forms adopted in the text. These make it possible to use compound interest to reduce continuous flows to scalars. Conceptually, given an endowment of K_0 and an initial wage w_0, the individual optimizes his preferences. I therefore define the indirect utility function $V^*(w_0, K_0)$ as the maximized value of the utility integral, that is,

$$V^*(w_0, K_0) = \max_{(h,s,K_T)} \int_0^T e^{-\rho t} [U(C) + V(L)] dt + B[(1-\tau)K_T]$$

subject to

$$\dot{K} = s,$$

$$C = rK + (w_0 e^{mt}) h - s.$$

Then, if K_0 is to be varied so as to compensate precisely for a change in w_0, the differentials must satisfy

$$dV^* = \frac{\partial V^*}{\partial w_0} dw_0 + \frac{\partial V^*}{\partial K_0} dK_0 = 0,$$

or

$$\frac{dK_0}{dw_0}\bigg|_{V^* = \text{const.}} = -\frac{\partial V^*/\partial w_0}{\partial V^*/\partial K_0}.$$

So what needs to be proven to establish (3.40) is

$$\frac{\partial V^*/\partial w_0}{\partial V^*/\partial K_0} = H. \tag{3.41}$$

As usual, the exact proof varies by case. I present the proof for the case where $r - m - \rho > 0$ and $0 < R < T$. The proof when either $R = 0$ or $R = T$ is essentially a degenerate case of the derivation to follow. The proof for $0 \leqslant S \leqslant T$ is different, but quite analogous.

First write down the expression for lifetime utility, called U^*:[14]

$$U^* = \int_0^T U(C(t)) e^{-\rho t} dt + \int_0^R V(L(t)) e^{-\rho t} dt + \int_R^T V(1) e^{-\rho t} dt$$

$$+ B[(1 - \tau) K_T].$$

This, of course, is a *functional* of the time paths $C(t)$ and $L(t)$, as well as the scalar K_T. Fortunately, in the convenient iso-elastic case, both of these time paths are exponential growth paths: $C(t) = C_0 e^{gt}$, $L(t) = L_0 e^{\gamma t}$. Therefore, U^* can be thought of as a *function* of C_0, L_0, R, and K_T. The total differential of this function is

$$dU^* = \frac{\partial U^*}{\partial C_0} dC_0 + \frac{\partial U^*}{\partial L_0} dL_0 + \frac{\partial U^*}{\partial R} dR + \frac{\partial U^*}{\partial K_T} dK_T. \tag{3.42}$$

The reader is spared the computations, but using some of the properties of the optimal path derived in subsections 3.3.2 and 3.4.3 it is possible to express each of the derivatives in (3.42) as a function of

14. V^* is the maximized value of U^*.

C_0 and R. The results are

$$\frac{\partial U^*}{\partial C_0} = U'(C_0)N(r-g,T) > 0,$$

$$\frac{\partial U^*}{\partial L_0} = U'(C_0)w_0 N(r-m-\gamma,R) > 0,$$

$$\frac{\partial U^*}{\partial R} = V(L_R)e^{-\rho R} - V(1)e^{-\rho R} = 0,$$

$$\frac{\partial U^*}{\partial K_T} = U'(C_0)e^{-rT} > 0.$$

Substituting all of these expressions into (3.42) gives the basic relation needed to prove (3.41):

$$dU^* = U'(C_0)[N(r-g,T)dC_0$$

$$+ w_0 N(r-m-\gamma,R)dL_0 + e^{-rT}dK_T]. \tag{3.43}$$

Consider first the response of maximized utility to a change in K_0; it affects utility through changes in the optimal choices of C_0, L_0, and K_T. Specifically by (3.43),

$$\frac{\partial V^*}{\partial K_0} = U'(C_0)\left[N(r-g,T)\frac{dC_0}{dK_0} + w_0 N(r-m-\gamma,R)\frac{dL_0}{dK_0} + e^{-rT}\frac{dK_T}{dK_0}\right].$$

I now refer to the expressions derived in the text of this chapter to evaluate the derivatives in the above expression. These can be written

$$\frac{dC_0}{dK_0} = -\gamma(\epsilon/\delta)C_0\frac{dR}{dK_0},$$

$$\frac{dL_0}{dK_0} = -\gamma L_0\frac{dR}{dK_0},$$

$$\frac{dK_T}{dK_0} = -\gamma(\epsilon/\beta)K_T\frac{dR}{dK_0}.$$

Substituting these three expressions and simplifying, it can be shown that

$$\frac{\partial V^*}{\partial K_0} = U'(C_0)[F'(R) - w_0 H'(R)]\frac{dR}{dK_0}.$$

Finally, referring to the expression for dR/dK_0 in the case at hand (see equation (3.37)) yields

$$\frac{\partial V^*}{\partial K_0} = U'(C_0).\qquad(3.44)$$

In words, the marginal increment to maximized utility attributable to an increase in inherited wealth is the marginal utility of initial consumption.

Now return to (3.42) and use it to evaluate dV^*/dw_0 in the same way:

$$\frac{\partial V^*}{\partial w_0} = U'(C_0)\left[N(r-g,T)\frac{dC_0}{dw_0} + w_0 N(r-m-\gamma,R)\frac{dL_0}{dw_0} + e^{-rT}\frac{dK_T}{dw_0}\right].$$

The relevant derivatives are

$$\frac{dC_0}{dw_0} = \frac{\partial C_0}{\partial w_0} + \frac{\partial C_0}{\partial R}\frac{dR}{dw_0},$$

$$\frac{dL_0}{dw_0} = -\gamma L_0\frac{dR}{dw_0},$$

$$\frac{dK_T}{dw_0} = \frac{\partial K_T}{\partial w_0} + \frac{\partial K_T}{\partial R}\frac{dR}{dw_0}.$$

Substitution of each of these and a considerable amount of manipulation results in

$$\frac{\partial V^*}{\partial w_0} = U'(C_0)H(R).$$

Equation (3.41) follows immediately from this and (3.44). Q.E.D.

4
Simulating the United States Income Distribution

And who does not know that to approach the question of economic equality is to enter a region haunted...by...'doleful voices and rushings to and fro', and the giant with a grim and surly voice, who shows pilgrims the skulls of those whom he has already despatched, and threatens to tear them also in pieces...

R.H. Tawney

The last two chapters dealt with the behavior of an individual maximizing unit, the family, and have only peripherally touched upon the income distribution question. I am now in a position to exploit this preliminary work by using the model of Chapters 2 and 3 as a building block in a simulation model of income distribution. The basic method is quite simple. Previous chapters have developed equations that show how—given a set of taste parameters, endowments of "skill" and capital, and certain characteristics of the economy—an individual plans his life cycle in consumption and labor supply. In particular, the model generates lifetime discounted earnings M as well as income at each age, $Y(t)$. By taking a hypothetical cohort of individuals with different tastes and different endowments, all of whom face the same economic environment, this apparatus can be used to generate a distribution of lifetime (or annual) incomes.

The first question with which I would like to confront the model is the basic question of this book: Can microeconomic theory—which I take to be based on the theory of maximizing behavior—explain the great inequality observed in the income distribution statistics of all capitalist nations? Karl Marx, in his challenge to capitalism, asked whether an *ideally functioning* capitalist economy could long survive. The spirit of this inquiry is similar. I posit the existence of a capitalistic United States with perfect markets everywhere. Borrowing and lending possibilities are unlimited for all persons. There is no involuntary unemployment. Except as it shows up in different wage rates for blacks and whites (or men and women) there is no discrimination.[1] Again, except as it shows up in differential wage rates, there is neither monopoly nor monopsony. Each individual faces a parametric wage and a parametric rate of return on capital, which he is powerless to influence. And I ask, Is such a perfectly competitive model capable of generating the degree of inequality observed in actual economies? The answer, as this chapter reveals, is yes. In fact, under what seem to be reasonable assumptions, the perfectly competitive model is capable of generating even more inequality than was observed in the United States in the 1960s.

The first step in such a simulation study is to create a synthetic "sample" of individuals. Although the method applies equally well to any capitalist system, I have designed the sample to imitate the U.S. economy of the 1960s. The manner in which this was done is explained in Sections 4.1–4.3.

Section 4.4 presents the basic simulation results and examines some of the salient characteristics of the synthetic economies. It is shown that, under a variety of assumptions, the simulation apparatus comes reasonably close to duplicating the behavior of the American economy. In particular, the lifetime income distribution estimates fall within the bounds suggested by the scanty available evidence. In fact, with no hard empirical evidence available, a simulation study such as this may well be the best way to "guesstimate" the distribution of lifetime incomes.

Having a synthetic economy to manipulate makes it possible to perform the *ceteris paribus* experiments that elude economists in the real world. Not only is there no factual evidence available on such questions as "How much inequality in incomes is attributable to inheritance?", but such questions may not be amenable to empirical answers *even in principle*. This is the strength of the simulation method, and, indeed, its main justification. Simulation can answer the hypothetical questions that enable us to tell how much of the observed inequality is attributable to tastes, how much to unequal wages, and so on. These results are presented in Chapter 5.

Chapter 6 uses the same simulation techniques to inquire into the effects of two widely discussed redistributional policies: proportional negative income taxes and proportional wage subsidies. Given the

1. In fact, the data suggest that differential wage rates do capture a great deal of the impact of race and sex discrimination. See Blinder [1973a] and subsection 5.2.2.

naïveté of the model, these experiments are perhaps as much illustrations of the usefulness of simulation techniques as they are statements about the likely effectiveness of these policies as redistributors. Nevertheless, the conclusions are sufficiently one-sided to be of interest.

4.1 Creating a Sample of Individuals

As readers of Chapters 2 and 3 will realize, an individual is identified by his wage rate at economic age zero, w_0; his inherited wealth K_0; and a set of six taste parameters, δ, ϵ, β, ξ, b, and ρ, which are the constants in the general utility functional

$$U^* = \int_0^T e^{-\rho t} \left[\frac{C(t)^{1-\delta}}{1-\delta} + \xi \frac{L(t)^{1-\epsilon}}{1-\epsilon} \right] dt + \frac{b^\beta [(1-\tau) K_T]^{1-\beta}}{1-\beta}. \quad (4.1)$$

Quite good data are available on wage rates, and some scanty data on inheritances are also available. Of course, there are no observations on tastes, so these had to be invented. Let me first consider the wage rates in the synthetic sample.

4.1.1 The Distribution of Wages
The theoretical variable w_0 corresponds to the wage rate earned at the start of an individual's working life. Actual micro-data from the cross-sectional panel used in the Survey Research Center's *A Panel Study of Income Dynamics*[2] were used for this purpose. These data have the important advantage of giving *actual observations* on hourly earnings (total labor income ÷ hours of work), whereas the Bureau of the Census computes its wage variable by dividing labor income during the previous year by the product of hours of work in the previous week times the number of weeks worked in the previous year. If the week prior to the Census survey was an "unusual" one—as it must be for some respondents—this can introduce serious errors.[3]

Of course, the hourly wage rate is not what is meant by w_0 in the theoretical model. Instead, w_0 is the *potential* earnings that could be obtained by an individual who worked every available hour during

2. For a description of this survey, see Survey Research Center [1970] or Morgan and Smith [1969].
3. For example, it can result in a serious underestimate of wages for any person who had some weeks of partial employment during the year.

the period. Since the model uses the year as the unit for measuring time and assumes that there are sixteen discretionary hours in each day (eight being needed for sleeping and eating), there are 16 hours/day × 7 days/week × 52 weeks/year = 5,864 hours/year available for work. Thus the w_0 for each person was obtained by multiplying the observed hourly wage by 5,864.

Since the theoretical variable is the wage rate at the start of the working career, a sample of 400 wage rates for heads of households between 25 and 29 years of age was drawn from the Survey Research Center (SRC) data. The highest wage rate in the group was $8.20 per hour, while the lowest was 14¢; the average wage was $2.60 per hour. To obtain some notion of the dispersion of wages, the Gini ratio was calculated and found to be 0.258. For purposes of comparison, Gini ratios for the U.S. income distribution generally fall in the 0.35–0.45 range. The distribution of wages used in the sample is summarized in Table 4.1.

4.1.2 The Distribution of Inherited Wealth
While there is a limited, but growing, bank of data on the distribution of wealth in the United States[4] these are not the data required for this study. The model calls for the distribution of *inherited* wealth, and there is a dearth of information on this subject. The Internal Revenue Service does publish distributions of estates subject to taxation; but estates *bequeathed* are not the same as inheritances *received*, and only estates in excess of $60,000 are subject to the federal estate tax. Since estates above $60,000 comprise only a fraction of the upper tail of the distribution, these data are of little use in constructing a distribution of inherited wealth for the nation as a whole.

The only data on the subject known to me are those collected by the Survey Research Center in its large survey of March 1960 and first reported by Morgan, David, Cohen, and Brazer [1962, p. 89]. These same data have recently been disaggregated by age group and further analyzed by Lansing and Sonquist [1969]. This disaggregation by age is quite important. Unlike the mythical world of perfect certainty and perfect capital markets, where it is valid to treat all inheritances *as if* they are received at age zero, in the real world inheritances tend to be received much later in life. To serve as the distribution of the theoretical variable K_0, then, I have chosen the

4. The best study is probably Projector and Weiss [1966]. See also French [1970] and Lansing and Sonquist [1969].

TABLE 4.1 DISTRIBUTION OF WAGES,
1967, AGES 25–29

Range	Relative Frequency
$0.14–$1.00	7.2%
1.00– 1.50	10.9%
1.50– 2.00	13.6%
2.00– 2.50	15.0%
2.50– 3.00	15.3%
3.00– 3.50	14.8%
3.50– 4.00	10.0%
4.00– 4.50	6.8%
4.50– 5.00	3.3%
5.00– 6.00	2.2%
6.00– 8.20	0.9%

Source: Survey Research Center tape (see text).

Note: As any actual sample of wages will include some variation due to purely transitory phenomena, the distribution given in the table may be thought to *overestimate* the dispersion in average lifetime wages. No attempt was made to correct for this.

TABLE 4.2 DISTRIBUTION OF INHERITED WEALTH, 1960,
HOUSEHOLDS WITH HEADS AGED 55–64 YEARS

Inheritance Received	Relative Frequency
Zero	72.3%
$ 1 – $ 449	4.0
450 – 949	1.2
950 – 4,949	10.1
4,950 – 9,949	5.4
9,950 – 24,949	4.3
24,950 and up	2.7

Source: Based on Lansing and Sonquist [1969, p. 64, Table 15].

Note: In the original data, inheritance was not ascertained for 2.6% of the sample. These persons were allocated to inheritance ranges in the same proportions as the 97.4% who answered the question.

distribution of inherited wealth in March 1960 of households with heads between 55 and 64 years of age. It was hoped that this age cohort was old enough to have received almost all inheritances from its parents, but not so old so that a significant number of them had already died. The distribution is presented in Table 4.2.

These data are plagued by several drawbacks, none of which can be remedied here. First, since the survey was not primarily designed to yield inheritance data, the size of the age 55–64 sample is rather small. With only 484 persons, representing 15.3% of the total sample, one may justifiably suspect that sampling variability is large. Second, as inspection of Table 4.2 reveals, the SRC made a very unfortunate selection of groups. Thus, the third cell ($450–949) is almost empty while the following cell ($950–4,949) contains nearly half of all persons receiving a positive inheritance. Finally, selecting $24,950 as the starting point for the open-ended top bracket conceals almost all the information about the shape of the upper tail of the distribution.

Still these are the only available data on which to base the distribution of K_0, so micro-data were fabricated to fit the distribution given by Table 4.2; that is, 289 families received no inheritance, 16 families received between $450 and $949, and so on. Within each bracket the distribution of inheritances was taken, for lack of a better assumption, to be approximately uniform. The upper bracket, of course, required special treatment. The highest eleven inheritances (2.7% of the total) were assumed to be $29,000; $39,000; $49,000; $59,000; $79,000; $99,000; $119,000; $179,000; $239,000; $359,000; and $479,000. Thus, while there are no Du Ponts in the sample, there are some quite substantial inherited fortunes.

One problem remains. I have actual data on the distribution of initial wages w_0 and inheritances K_0 but no direct information on the association of wages with inheritances in the real world. Casual empiricism suggests that there is positive correlation between K_0 and w_0 (since both are, at least partially, reflections of the economic status of the parents), but offers no clue as to how strong this correlation is. Since there is no way to settle this question on a priori grounds, several different assumptions were made. In what I shall call *the egalitarian society* (Regime I), the extreme assumption that w_0 and K_0 are uncorrelated is made. This signifies a milieu of great equality of opportunity where the fact that one received a large inheritance is unrelated to one's adult productivity. All persons in this world have equal access to the educational system. In fact, Regime I is even more egalitarian than this. If one's parents were able to leave a large estate at least partly because they were of high ability, it must be the case *either* that none of this ability has been genetically transmitted to the offspring, *or* that the wage rate is independent of ability.[5]

One strongly suspects, although there is no hard statistical evidence, that w_0 and K_0 are in fact positively correlated. But how strongly? In simulating a society with *inequality of opportunity* (Regime II), it is assumed that $r(w_0, K_0)$ is positive and two different values are tried: $+0.26$ and $+0.51$.[6] It should be noted that since most of the K_0 values are zero, a correlation with w_0 of 0.26 is quite substantial, and a correlation of 0.51 is more extreme than has probably ever characterized the U.S. economy, as it represents nearly perfect correlation within that part of the population which has inheritances. Thus, if either of these cases is relevant to the American economy, it is probably the more moderate correlation. In any case, experimenting with both values in the simulation runs gives some idea as to how sensitive inequality is to this parameter.

4.1.3 The Distribution of Tastes
Real world data reveal little about the distribution of tastes. The utility function (4.1) has six parameters which could conceivably vary across individuals: ρ indicates the rate of subjective time discounting; ξ and b indicate the relative weights attached to leisure and bequests, respectively (as compared to consumption, whose weight is unity); δ, ϵ, and β indicate the speeds at which the marginal utilities of consumption, leisure, and bequests decline as their respective quantities rise.

The last three parameters play crucial roles in determining the wealth elasticities of each good and were arbitrarily taken to be invariant across individuals. Since there is no strong evidence that leisure is either a luxury good or its opposite, it was decided to make $\delta = \epsilon$, thus making the wealth elasticities of leisure and consumption approximately equal. Bequests, however, are presumably a luxury good, so it was decided to set $\beta < \delta$. As mentioned in Chapter 3, when $\delta = \epsilon = 1$, the instantaneous utility function becomes a Cobb-Douglas function with weighting factors $1/(1 + \xi)$ for consumption

---

5. The view that only education, and not ability apart from education, determines wage rates has been propounded recently by Bowles [1972] and Gintis [1971]. See also Griliches [1970] and Griliches and Mason [1972]. Some evidence that ability does matter, at least for educated persons, is presented by Hause [1972] and Taubman and Wales [1973].

6. The reasons for choosing these values are explained in subsection 4.4.2.

and $\xi/(1+\xi)$ for leisure. Since the basic behavior patterns when $\delta = \epsilon$ are the same regardless of their common value, and since using the Cobb-Douglas form makes the interpretation of ξ so easy, it was decided to adopt $\delta = \epsilon = 1$ for simulation purposes. The remaining elasticity β was set equal to two-thirds, making the wealth elasticity of bequests approximately equal to $1\frac{1}{2}$.[7] There is no empirical evidence on this elasticity, but examination of the simulation results indicated that $1\frac{1}{2}$ gave a plausible distribution of bequests.

The remaining taste parameters were permitted to vary from person to person. In each case a normal distribution was adopted for no better reason than that *physical* traits of individuals have been found to obey the Gaussian probability law.

Once the Cobb-Douglas form had been adopted, it was a simple matter to pick the mean value for ξ. Of the 5,864 hours per year available for work, the typical person chooses to devote about 2,000 to work and the remainder to leisure.[8] That is, he uses about $3,864/5,864 = 0.66$ of his available time for leisure. Since the weight in the Cobb-Douglas utility function for leisure is $\xi/(1+\xi)$, the mean value of ξ was chosen to satisfy $E(\xi)/E(1+\xi) = 0.66$.[9] The standard deviation for ξ was arbitrarily set to 0.6 in order to make values of ξ very close to zero (or even negative) extremely unlikely while allowing considerable dispersion in tastes.[10]

The distribution of ρ, the subjective rate of time discounting, was also given the Gaussian form. Since Chapter 3 revealed that the life cycle in labor and leisure is *qualitatively* different depending on whether $r - m$ is greater or less than ρ, $E(\rho)$ was set equal to $r - m$ so as to give approximately equal numbers of cases of each kind. The standard deviation of ρ was set to be one-third of the mean, which again allowed considerable dispersion in tastes while limiting the likelihood of getting a negative drawing from the normal distribution.[11] Since there is no particular reason to believe that $E(\rho) = r - m$, several experimental simulations were run with $E(\rho)$ placed either above or below $r - m$, and with different standard deviations. While

7. The wealth elasticity of bequests is approximately δ/β.
8. Clearly there are institutional reasons for such a choice. But these institutions presumably arose because people *wanted* a 40-hour work week. Furthermore, my goal in fixing a distribution of tastes is to imitate the behavior of the U.S. economy, and the institutional constraints do not appear elsewhere in the model.
9. Although $E[\xi/(1+\xi)] \neq E(\xi)/E(1+\xi)$, this refinement was not felt worth making.
10. When the random number generator produced values for ξ below zero, the parameter was arbitrarily set to $+0.05$. This occurred in only one case.
11. When a negative drawing was made, ρ was arbitrarily set to 0.0005. There was only one such case.

the behavior of individual families was found to be quite sensitive to ρ, overall statistics for the entire economy of 400 families were remarkably invariant.

The final taste parameter is b, the relative weight given to the bequest in the utility function. There is little intuition that can be brought to bear here. Although another investigator might well have completely different predilections, I selected the mean and standard deviation of b to (1) give a reasonable number of persons with no bequest motive at all;[12] (2) make tastes for bequests more disperse than labor-leisure tastes or time preferences; (3) make the average level of bequests exceed the average level of inheritance because of the growth of the economy and the slippage (estate taxes, funeral expenses, lawyer's fees, and the like) between the fortune bequeathed and the fortune actually received by heirs. After some experimentation, it was found that $E(b) = \sigma(b) = 0.25$ gave a plausible distribution for K_T.

4.1.4 The Question of Taste Formation

Once a trio of taste parameters, ξ, ρ, and b is generated for each of the 400 individuals, the remaining problem is to assign these tastes to persons. This raises some interesting, and quite fundamental, questions about the nature of taste formation. Are tastes "God-given" and independent of the economic circumstances in which a person grows up? If not, are they (at least partially) determined by economic circumstances, as represented in the model by the endowments of w_0 and K_0? Or are they correlated wth the parents' tastes? These are not questions that can be given definitive answers. My purpose here is simply to explore some of the issues and explain the arbitrary choices I made.

First, as some results in the next chapter make clear, the distributions of the parameters ρ and b turn out to have negligible impacts on inequality. Thus, in considering whether or not tastes should be correlated or independent, I shall worry only about the labor-leisure taste parameter ξ. Also, since ρ and b have such little impact on inequality, I shall not be concerned with any possible correlations among the three taste parameters.

Second, as indicated in Chapter 1, the intergenerational aspects of the simulation model have not been pursued here. For this reason, I have not dealt with the possibility that individuals' tastes are corre-

---

12. When the random number generator gave negative b values, b was truncated to zero.

lated with the tastes of their parents (as a special case of this, individuals might inherit their parents' tastes). It is quite plausible that some such correlation exists; and if it is substantial it serves as a transmitter of inequality across generations. For example, people with a high preference for consumption over leisure would pass on *both* money *and* the desire to earn more to their offspring.

This leaves only two possibilities: ξ might be correlated with w_0 or with K_0.

The question of whether or not tastes are independent is an ancient one in economics, and a very deep one. The hypothesis of exogenous tastes is one of the many places in which current economic theory is under incessant attack from the radical left. If microeconomic theory is the theory of maximizing behavior, and if preferences are themselves generated by the economic mechanism, nothing is left of normative economics and positive economics is dealt a near-fatal blow.

Of course, no economist believes that immutable tastes are given to each individual at birth. Tastes are certainly influenced by the social system, of which the economic system is a major part. It is simply that no economist—and, it might be added, no sociologist or psychologist either—has a very clear conception of how tastes are formed. Certainly there is no good analytical model of taste formation; and, until such a model is available, the case for treating tastes as exogenous is a powerful one. There is, after all, a great deal of variation in human behavior. Virtually every cross-sectional study of individuals shows that people who are identical in every measureable dimension, nevertheless behave differently. So one plausible maintained hypothesis is that tastes, and in particular the parameter ξ, are distributed independently of both w_0 and K_0. In simulation runs for the egalitarian society (Regime I) and inequality of opportunity (Regime II), this will be the working hypothesis.

While the principle of insufficient reason may argue for the assumption of independence, there is a huge store of anecdotal evidence about American society which argues for a negative correlation. As regards the lower tail of the distribution, the whole notion of the "psychology of poverty," as popularized, say, by Michael Harrington's *The Other America* [1962], suggests that despair, hopelessness, and low aspirations are part of the inheritance of the poor. At the opposite pole, such notions as "middle-class virtures," and the "keep-up-with-the-Joneses" syndrome suggest that being born into a more prosperous environment alters one's tastes in favor of hard work and high consumption, rather than the reverse.

The discussion thus far applies only to the tastes one is born with.[13] An entirely separate issue is how these tastes may change in response to economic events during one's lifetime. I shall not venture here into a discussion of the thorny issues surrounding the notion of endogenously changing tastes.[14] But it is not too difficult to incorporate into the simulation apparatus the notion that being born into favorable economic circumstances biases one's tastes in favor of consumption over leisure by altering the ξ parameters so that they are negatively correlated with w_0 or with K_0. In what follows *the programmed society* (called Regime III) refers to a milieu where K_0 is uncorrelated with w_0 (as in the egalitarian society), but where ξ is correlated with both. A person who finds the anecdotal evidence cited above persuasive may feel fairly certain that this correlation is negative, but, to investigate the equalizing effects of the reverse case, some positive correlations are also experimented with.

Of course, any actual economy might be characterized by both correlated tastes and a positive correlation between w_0 and K_0. Since there is no particular reason to believe that the disequalizing effects of correlated tastes and correlated wages are additive, I shall also consider a *stratified society* (Regime IV) where both correlations are present simultaneously. This regime stands at the opposite end of the spectrum from Regime I as the most inegalitarian milieu of all.

For the convenience of the reader, the defining characteristics of the four regimes to be considered in the remainder of this book are summarized in Table 4.3.

TABLE 4.3 DEFINING CHARACTERISTICS OF THE FOUR REGIMES

	Assumption about Labor-Leisure Tastes	
Assumption about Wages	Uncorrelated with w_0 or K_0	Correlated with w_0 and K_0
Uncorrelated with K_0	Regime I The egalitarian society	Regime III The programmed society
Correlated with K_0	Regime II Inequality of opportunity	Regime IV The stratified society

13. I mean, of course, "born" in the economic sense; say, at age eighteen.
14. The only formal paper on the subject known to me really deals wth remembering and forgetting what are essentially unchanged tastes over one's lifetime. See Weizsäcker [1971].

4.2 Specification of the Economic Environment

To complete the specification of the simulation model, it remains only to select values for those constants which appeared in Chapters 2 and 3 as characteristics of the economic environment into which the individuals are thrust. These parameters are—
1. r^*, the before-tax rate of interest, assumed the same for every person, whether a borrower or a lender;
2. m, the trend rate of growth of real wage rates;
3. T, the length of economic life;
4. u, the rate of proportional income taxation;
5. τ, the rate of proportional estate or inheritance taxation.

Some effort was made to select values for these five parameters that accurately represented the U.S. economy during the 1960s. However, picking real-world counterparts to theoretical constructs is always a tricky business, and there is nothing sacred about the particular choices made. With one exception (see below), the model was run with alternative values for every parameter. While individual behavior often changed quite dramatically, the impact on inequality was almost always trivial.

First consider r^*, the before-tax rate of interest. The interest rate here plays the dual role it always plays in models with perfect capital markets: it is simultaneously the rate of return earned on invested wealth and the rate at which future income streams are discounted. There is, of course, no such thing as "the" rate of interest to which I can turn for guidance in setting r^*, and rates of return have fluctuated substantially during the 1960s. As some sort of weighted average of the real rates of return on equities and fixed-income securities in the U.S. economy (which happens also to be the yield on long-term time deposits which has prevailed for the past several years), I have selected $r^* = 0.06$.

I have no desire to defend this essentially arbitrary decision, but two points are worth noting. First, I have not experimented wth different values of r^* simply because it is mainly the *difference*, $r^*(1-u)-m$, that matters; and I have experimented extensively with alternative choices for m. Second, and most importantly, I have assumed throughout that r^* is independent of u, that is, the pretax rate of return is independent of the income tax rate. Thus, in simulation runs where u is changed, the after-tax rate of return—and thus the discount rate—changes accordingly. I do not pretend that this extreme resolution of the shifting question (zero shifting) is accurate; I only contend that the small changes in r^* likely to accompany an alteration in tax rates are negligible enough to be ignored. Put differently, the model really deals only with the *supply of investible funds* which would be forthcoming at a given pretax return. Nothing is said about the *demand for capital*; and this, of course, tacitly assumes an accommodating demand response to stabilize the before-tax rate of return.[15]

The second important aspect of the economic environment is the trend rate of increase in real wages. What is the real-world counterpart to this concept? Recall that the model assumes that an individual receives a wage that grows exponentially at rate m. This, of course, is a compounding of two effects, since *both* age *and* calendar time increase annually by one year. Conceptually, if the wage rate is considered to be a function of both age A (due to seniority, experience, and the like), and calendar time t (due to technological improvements not embodied in the worker), $w = w(A,t)$, the desired growth rate is

$$m = \frac{1}{w} \frac{\partial w}{\partial A} \bigg|_{t=\text{const.}} + \frac{1}{w} \frac{\partial w}{\partial t} \bigg|_{A=\text{const.}}.$$

The first term on the right-hand side is the effect of age on wages, calendar time held constant. Empirically, this would be the age trend observed in cross-sectional studies at a point in time; call it m_1. The second term is the general growth of wage levels over time, age held constant; call it m_2. Then, $m = m_1 + m_2$. My own cross-sectional study of individual wage rates suggests that there is almost no noticeable *linear* cross-sectional age trend in the logarithm of wages; that is, $m_1 \approx 0$. Wages tend to rise at a declining rate until the middle forties, and fall thereafter. By the age of retirement, they are only about 5% higher than their levels at age eighteen.[16] This means that m is equal to m_2, the general time trend in the level of wages. For this purpose I have used the compound rate of growth of real wages over the decade 1960–1970, as given in the *Economic Report of the President, 1971*, which was 1.64% per annum.[17]

---

15. This is analogous to the treatment of the labor market, where the model deals only with the supply side. Clearly a general equilibrium treatment of both sides of each market would be preferable, but is beyond the scope of this study.

16. Blinder [1971]. Specifically, in a regression to explain the logarithm of w, the coefficients of age were: $0.0277A - 0.00032A^2$.

17. The wage series used was "average gross hourly earnings in private nonagricultural industry," Table C-29, p. 231; deflated by the consumer price index, Table C-46, p. 250.

Of course, since people live to different ages, there is no real-world counterpart to parameter T, the length of economic life. As a simple solution, I have given everybody the life expectancy of the average individual who reaches "economic age zero."[18] As stated earlier, I have taken bioloical age eighteen to correspond to economic age zero. According to the 1970 *Statistical Abstract of the United States*,[19] the life expectancy of an American surviving to age eighteen in 1967 was 54.7 years, that is, to age 72.7. Thus $T = 54.7$ was used in the simulations. Some experiments with $T = 60$ were also tried, and the results were not very different.

Chapters 2 and 3 make it clear that the only taxes that can readily be incorporated into the model are proportional ones. This does not do a great injustice to the personal income tax, which is not nearly so progressive as the statute books indicate; but, as shown in Section 2.5, it does give a somewhat distorted view of the federal estate tax. However, since the estate tax itself is relatively unimportant it was not thought that this introduced much error. Since each tax is to be treated as if it were administered at a flat rate with no exemption, the appropriate real-world counterparts would appear to be the observed ratios of tax receipts/tax base. For the federal estate tax, this ratio was 0.134 in 1965,[20] and we shall proceed "as if" this applied also to estates of less than $60,000. For the income tax, the 1970 edition of *Statistics of Income* indicated that the ratio of personal income tax receipts to income subject to tax was 0.218 on 1968 returns.[21] It may occur to the reader that the income tax surcharge was in effect during part of 1968. But since Waldorf's study [1967] indicates slightly higher effective rates throughout the 1960s without the surcharge, the 0.218 figure was not adjusted downward. In any case, results reported in the next chapter indicate that small errors in either effective tax rate do not affect the simulated income distribution.

---

18. It is, of course, possible in simulations to duplicate the U.S. mortality experience by assigning different, but *known*, T's to each person. This was not thought worth the effort. By contrast, to allow T to be stochastic, a different model is needed. Yaari's [1965] results previously cited, however, suggest that consumer behavior would not be much affected if life insurance were available in unlimited amounts. While not altering consumption and labor supply behavior very markedly, death at unexpected times would have a notable impact on the distribution of bequests.

19. Table 67, page 54.

20. The simulations were run before the latest estate tax data, reported in Table 2.1, were available. This is why 0.134 is used as the tax rate instead of 0.136.

21. Table 3.7, p. 109.

4.3 A Note on Methodology

Unlike the various branches of statistical investigation, the appropriate techniques for model verification and hypothesis testing are not at all well developed for simulation studies. Naturally, any investigator will hesitate to draw inferences from his simulation model until he is relatively satisfied that it "works." Thus there is inevitably a certain amount of fiddling with parameter values to make the simulation results come out looking realistic. Given this, it is hard to know to what extent the conclusions that emerge might have been "cooked." The analogy to the problem of data mining in econometrics is clear enough.

Since, in the design of a simulation apparatus, there are always subjective judgements to be made, there is simply no way of circumventing this problem. To continue the analogy, one suspects that very few published regression studies report the version of the estimating equation which first emerged from the author's computer. To expect more from designers of simulation experiments would be patently unreasonable. While the problem cannot be eliminated, I have adopted a set of methodological guidelines designed to minimize its importance.

First, I attempted to pare down the number of subjective choices that had to be made. Where a parameter could be obtained from actual U.S. data, it was obtained and used in the simulations regardless of the results. The distributions of wages and inheritances, the values of the two tax rates, the trend rate of growth of real wages and the length of economic life were all settled upon in this way.

Second, where the facts cannot adjudicate the question, by far the best procedure would appear to be to run the simulation model and report the results under alternative specifications of the parameter at issue. The danger here is that, if there are more than a few such parameters and/or the number of trial values for each is large, the number of posssible combinations quickly becomes so staggering that the reader—if not, indeed, the investigator himself—finds himself lost in a maze of results which he is unable to digest and synthesize. Thus only for the intercorrelations among wages, inheritances, and tastes did I adopt the procedure of running the model under several alternative parameter values. (These choices define the four regimes.)

This leaves open the most difficult question: what to do about those parameters that cannot simply be observed in the real world and that are not accorded the treatment described in the preceding paragraph. In the present study, this set included the rate of interest and the distributions of all the taste parameters. My resolution of this dilemma was to experiment with alternative choices until one was found which gave reasonable results, but in so doing to blind myself to those conclusions in which I was primarily interested. More concretely, this book is concerned with the size distribution of earnings and incomes; but the output of the simulation model includes many other features of the U.S. economy as well, for example, labor's share in national income. My procedure was consistently to "fit" the model to these other features, without looking at the ramifications for the income distribution.

The choice of the mean value of b, the relative preference for bequests, illustrates the idea well. A little reflection will show that labor's share in national income might be quite sensitive to the choice of $E(b)$. With a high preference for bequests, individuals accumulate a great deal of nonhuman wealth and thus there is considerable property income; conversely, with little liking for bequests, there is less property income. This makes it possible to select a value of $E(b)$ so as to make labor's share in the simulated economy come out reasonably close to labor's actual share, without considering what bearing this choice might have on the size distribution of lifetime income.[22] To follow this method consistently, solutions to individual life cycles were computed and printed out, but the income distribution was not tabulated, during the "model fitting" stage. Furthermore, in this particular study I had the "advantage" that no one really knows what the lifetime income distribution looks like. So "goodness of fit" could only be appraised by looking at the distribution of annual incomes. Since the model was calibrated and the entire analysis carried out on the basis of lifetime incomes, there appears to be little danger that the close correspondence between actual and predicted *annual* income distributions reported in Section 5.3 is due to "cooking."

4.4 Simulating the Distribution of Lifetime Incomes

Some portion of the observed inequality in annual incomes is surely attributable to life-cycle influences that "wash out" when the unit of time is taken to be the lifetime. For the U.S., however, there are no

22. Some economists would, I believe, argue that making labor's share come out right loads the dice in favor of the size distribution coming out right. My own opinion (which was borne out by the simulation results), however, is that the correspondence between the size distribution and relative factor shares is none too tight.

reliable data on the lifetime income distribution because of the obvious difficulty of following an age cohort through a long period of time. It is thus impossible to measure directly the inequality of lifetime incomes; the best that can be done empirically is to make some crude guesses based on the work of other investigators.

Irving Kravis [1962] has tabulated income data for the same panel of households over a five-year period 1949, 1951–1954. He found that while the Gini ratios for single years ranged from 0.31 to 0.33, the Gini ratio for average income over the five-year period was 0.29, about 10% less. Using the coefficient of variation as his measure, Kravis found annual inequality ranging between 0.61 and 0.66 while inequality over a five-year period was only 0.56.[23] Although income tax laws typically use a less-than-ideal definition of income, a better data source may be the continuous sample of Delaware income tax returns over 1925–1936. The average single-year Gini ratio over this period was 0.467, and the ratio for the full 12-year period was 0.432 [Kravis, 1962, p. 272], which is only about 8% lower. For Norway, there are somewhat more reliable data. Lee Soltow's detailed study of the distributional history of the city of Sarpsborg shows that while the annual Gini ratios over 1928–1960 averaged 0.183, the 33-year Gini ratio for the same sample was only 0.134, a full 27% less [Soltow, 1965, Exhibit 55, p. 102].

The only serious attempt to estimate the lifetime income distribution in the U.S. known to me is Robert Summers' unpublished study [1956]. Summers, lacking actual lifetime data for a group of individuals, fit age-specific difference equations of the form $\log Y_t = a + b \log Y_{t-1}$ to data on earnings in successive years for a panel of individuals. Then, assuming that the equations estimated for 1950–1951 held over an entire lifetime, he generated a hypothetical distribution of lifetime earnings. Frederic Pryor [1969, p. 30] calculated a Gini coefficient of 0.21 from these data, and Summers calculated a coefficient of variation of 0.404. There are two idiosyncrasies of Summers' study that should be noted. First, he considers *earnings* instead of income. Perhaps the Gini coefficient including property income would be higher, perhaps not. Second, his definition of lifetime income is the total of *undiscounted* earnings over a 40-year period. It is not clear what effect the interest rate (which Summers takes to be zero) should have on the Gini ratio, but using undiscounted earnings seems an odd procedure.

23. Kravis [1962, pp. 269–271] notes that this panel probably understates inequality since blacks, single-person households, and unskilled workers are underrepresented in the sample.

Finally, there has been one previous attempt to simulate the U.S. distribution of earnings (not income) by Ray Fair [1971]. Fair's specific techniques differ widely from my own, and his concern is to simulate the *optimal* degree of inequality (defined by maximizing a symmetric social welfare function subject to behavioral constraints) rather than the *actual*. Still his results may be of some interest here. His most reasonable specifications of an earnings function yield lifetime Gini ratios for earnings ranging from 0.209 to 0.264 with identical tastes, and from 0.304 to 0.336 with very disperse tastes.

Based on these sources, one might hazard a guess—in which I place no particular confidence—that the Gini ratio for lifetime income is approximately 0.25–0.30. With somewhat more confidence, one might surmise that the range 0.20 to 0.35 brackets the true Gini value. In view of the difficulties involved in learning the lifetime income distribution from the "facts," simulation may well be the best way to remove life-cycle influences from the distribution.

The present section reports the results obtained with the model described in the preceding sections of this chapter. As previously explained, I have chosen to investigate a number of regimes corresponding to different assumptions about the intercorrelations among wages, inheritances, and labor-leisure tastes.

4.4.1 The Egalitarian Society (Regime I)
The measure of lifetime income employed throughout this study is the present discounted value of lifetime earnings over the 54.7 year lifetime, plus the inheritance (which is already in present value terms), that is $K_0 + M$. Readers of Chapter 3 will recall that the lifetime budget constraint equates the sum of the discounted present values of lifetime consumption and bequest to $K_0 + M$; so $K_0 + M$ is a reasonable welfare measure.[24]

Table 4.4 gives the distribution of lifetime incomes resulting from the simulation when w_0, K_0, and ξ are all mutually independent. The Gini ratio for the distribution is 0.295 while the Gini ratio for

24. The indirect lifetime utility function has as its main arguments K_0 and w_0. There is no rigorously "correct" way to reduce these two arguments to a single number. One possibility would be to weight the wage by *potential hours* and thereby calculate lifetime "full income," $K_0 + w_0 N(r - m, T)$. Another possibility (the one adopted here) is to weight the wage according to *actual hours* worked, and thereby compute actual lifetime income: $K_0 + w_0 H$. In terms of the simple atemporal budget diagram shown in Figure 4.1, the first procedure entails representing the budget line by point F, while the second uses point A instead.

TABLE 4.4 DISTRIBUTION OF $K_0 + M$: THE EGALITARIAN
SOCIETY (REGIME I)

Population Group		Approximate Income Range	Share in Total
Lowest	10%	$ 8,000– 48,000	2.78%
Second	10%	48,000– 64,500	4.67
Third	10%	64,500– 82,000	6.06
Fourth	10%	82,000– 99,000	7.31
Fifth	10%	99,000–112,000	8.58
Sixth	10%	112,000–128,000	9.77
Seventh	10%	128,000–145,500	11.19
Eighth	10%	145,500–167,500	12.73
Ninth	10%	167,500–206,000	15.39
Highest	10%	206,000–560,000	21.52
Top	5%	237,500– 560,000	12.65
Top	1%	378,500–560,000	3.69

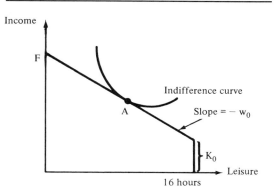

Figure 4.1

earnings alone is 0.300.[25] Using the coefficient of variation, however, inequality in $K_0 + M$ exceeds inequality in M alone by 0.562 to 0.545. These figures at least cast doubt on the glib assertion, too often heard, that earnings are much more equally distributed than income as a whole. What *is* certainly true is that earnings are much more equally distributed than property income. But, owing to the disincentive effects of property income on work effort, it is quite possible for *both* labor income and property income to be less equally distributed than their sum. That this possibility is a real one is illustrated in the present simulation by the observed sample correlation of -0.114 between M and K_0. Also, a recent study by Projector, Weiss, and Thoresen [1969, p. 111], which separately tabulated labor and property incomes, found a concentration ratio of 0.43 for total income resulting from ratios of 0.52 for labor income and 0.93 for property income.

Before examining the distribution of income in other regimes, it is worth pausing to see how accurately the simulation apparatus depicts the actual American economy, that is, how the simulated capital-labor ratio, average earnings, effective tax burden, and other nondistributional aspects compare with their real-world counterparts. As mentioned above, the model was designed to fit those facts as accurately as possible.

Average lifetime discounted earnings after-tax in the synthetic sample are $116,637. By way of comparison, a person earning $2.60 per hour (the sample mean) at age eighteen who worked 2,000 hours per year for his entire remaining 54.7 years of life, and whose wages grew at 1.64% per annum, would have had lifetime discounted earnings of $134,502 before tax and $105,181 after a 21.8% income tax.[26] The figure of $116,637 after taxes seems quite reasonable by comparison. There are, of course, no empirical data with which to compare the simulation results since the age cohorts which were 18–29 years of age during the 1960s still have the better part of their working lives ahead of them.

As has been mentioned, the model contains only the supply sides of the labor and capital markets, and therefore is exceedingly partial.

---

25. Gini ratios were calculated in the usual way, that is, by numerical integration under a piecewise-linear approximation to the Lorenz curve. It is well known that this method systematically understates inequality. However, in a recent study critical of this technique, Gastwirth [1972] shows that if the number of groups is large (say 25 or more), the error is quite small. Since I used 40 groups in all Gini calculations, I surmise that the bias is no more than 0.001 or 0.002 and is probably less than that.
26. The discount rate used in these calculations is $0.06(1-0.218)=0.0469$.

Nevertheless it is of interest to see how the implied capital intensity of the simulated economy compares with the facts. The reader should note that, unlike some other simulation studies, no particular value of labor's share has been built into the model by, say, assuming a Cobb-Douglas aggregate production function. Households are perfectly free to supply as much labor and demand as much capital as they please. In the model, the share of property income in total income turns out to be 15.4%. This seems slightly low, but not drastically out of line with actual U.S. factor shares. The most comparable empirical data would seem to be the composition of adjusted gross income on individual income tax returns, since this is how the factor share calculation was made in the simulated economy. For 1967, according to *Statistics of Income—1968*,[27] the share of all income other than wages and salaries in total adjusted gross income was 18.5%. Since this includes capital gains, which do not exist in the model, and income of unincorporated businesses, some of which is certainly a return to labor, I feel relatively satisfied by this comparison.

Another comparison concerns the overall tax burden. In the simulation, if the sum of the inheritance plus discounted earnings before tax is taken as the tax base, then income and estate taxes together absorb 25.6% of this base. That this matches quite closely the actual burden of federal taxation in the U.S. is no surprise in view of the manner in which I selected the two tax rates.

Another nondistributional characteristic of the sample is the propensity of the workers to withdraw entirely from the labor force during some stage in their life cycle. Of the 400 individuals, only 50 persons choose to take some of their 54.7 available years in the form of retirement. It is hard to tell how "realistic" this is. Retirement in the model means retirement on one's own savings, with neither pension benefits nor social security payments above one's own previous contributions. Also, death in the model comes at age 72.7, so retirement means retiring before this age. I would not venture to guess whether more or fewer than one person in eight would voluntarily retire before age 73 under these circumstances if part-time work (in any small amount and at a high wage) were always available, but the small number of retirees does not seem unreasonable in this light. It should be noted here that the number of persons choosing retirement is quite sensitive to the trend rate of increase in wages; at $m = 0$ many more leave the labor force with advancing age.

27. U.S. Internal Revenue Service [1970], Table 1A, page 2.

Also, as anticipated in Section 3.3, persons who take "retirement" at the start of life are rather less prone to choose a retirement period than those who take retirement late in life.

One question concerning the value of the simulation apparatus which has not been addressed so far is this: How much of the inequality in the simulated income distribution is just the result of mechanically combining the vectors w_0 and K_0, and how much is attributable to the labor-leisure and consumption-savings decisions which the model seeks to explicate?

My procedure for answering this question was straightforward, though the interpretation of the results may not be. In an economy of automatons, with no behavioral responses, every person would work a fixed number of hours and therefore earnings would be strictly proportional to wage rates. The lifetime income distribution would be obtained by adding inheritances to these mechanically computed earnings. When I did this, assuming each person spent 2,000 hours at work each year, I obtained a Gini ratio of 0.269 for lifetime income, $K_0 + M$. The distribution of earnings alone, of course, displayed precisely the same inequality as the distribution of wage rates, a Gini ratio of 0.258. By contrast, when the behavioral aspects are considered, the simulation apparatus raises the Gini ratios to 0.295 for income and 0.300 for earnings.

What, then, does this say about the "explanatory power" of the model? Clearly the mechanical procedure already accounts for most of the inequality in either earnings or incomes; that is, 0.269 is much closer to 0.295 than to zero. But is zero inequality the relevant frame of reference? I think not. If, instead, one views the model as designed to explain the amount by which the Gini ratio exceeds 0.258 (the Gini ratio for wages), one may feel relatively satisfied in that behavioral responses account for 70% of the difference.

4.4.2 Inequality of Opportunity (Regime II)
The reader will recall that imparting some positive correlation between w_0 and K_0 is my crude way of modeling the notion that offspring of rich families tend to have access to more and better education, better "contacts," and the like, and therefore earn higher wages as adults. The procedure followed in simulating this regime is to re-assign the inheritances to persons in such a way as to make w_0 and K_0 correlated. To obtain a positive correlation of 0.26 (referred to below as Regime IIa), it is only necessary to reassign the 111 positive inheritances among the 111 persons receiving a positive

inheritance so as to create perfect rank correlation within this group. I imagine that the actual correlation is no higher than this, and probably lower. To simulate the effect of extreme inequality of opportunity (Regime IIb), the 111 positive inheritances are taken from this group and assigned to the highest 111 wages in the sample with perfect rank correlation. This makes the sample correlation between w_0 and K_0 about 0.51. Summary statistics for the income distributions in Regime II are presented in Table 4.5 where the corresponding data for Regime I are repeated for comparison.

Examination of this table is quite enlightening. It is dramatically clear from lines 2 and 3 that even quite substantial positive correlation between inheritance and productivity does not increase inequality very much. Lines 4–6 reveal the reason for this surprising result. When a positive correlation between w_0 and K_0 is introduced (or increased), there are two opposing forces at work. On the one hand, such correlation destroys the negative covariance between inherited wealth and earnings which exists in the egalitarian society due to disincentive effects of lump-sum income. The correlation goes from -0.114 in Regime I to $+0.035$ in Regime IIb, causing an increase in inequality. However, these same work disincentives lead to a coun-

TABLE 4.5 COMPARISON OF THE EGALITARIAN SOCIETY WITH INEQUALITY OF OPPORTUNITY

Characteristic	Egalitarian Society Regime I	Inequality of Opportunity	
		Regime IIa	Regime IIb
(1) $r(w_0, K_0)$	0	0.26	0.51
Inequality of $K_0 + M$			
(2) (a) Gini Ratio	0.295	0.300	0.300
(3) (b) Coeff. of Variation	0.562	0.579	0.570
Inequality of M			
(4) (a) Gini Ratio	0.300	0.288	0.278
(5) (b) Coeff. of Variation	0.545	0.526	0.508
(6) $r(K_0, M)$	-0.114	0.012	0.035
(7) Labor's Share	0.846	0.847	0.847
(8) Federal Tax Burden	0.256	0.255	0.255
(9) Average Lifetime Earnings	$116,637	$116,270	$115,758
(10) Number of Retirees	50	43	45

tervailing decrease in the inequality in M since persons with high wages (who are more likely to be high earners) also receive substantial inheritances. This phenomenon is graphically revealed in lines 4 and 5. The result of these two conflicting forces is a minor increase in inequality when $r(w_0, K_0)$ rises from zero to 0.26, and no further increase when $r(w_0, K_0)$ rises again to its maximal value. These results again underscore the strength of the simulation method. In theoretical work, when one comes across two conflicting forces, one can generally say no more than the inevitable "it all depends." Simulation allows the investigator to get a grip on the relative magnitudes of the two (or more) countervailing tendencies, so that important questions can be given at least tentative answers.

Perusal of lines 7–10 will convince the reader that the salient nondistributional aspects of the economy are not much affected in going from the egalitarian society to inequality of opportunity. The only discernible trend is that fewer persons retire in Regime II. The reason for this is simply that some low wage individuals, who would normally retire, are induced to remain in the labor force by the loss of their inherited wealth.

4.4.3 The Programmed Society (Regime III)

The defining characteristic of the programmed society, as the reader will recall, is that poor people (i.e., people with low productivity and/or low inheritances) tend to be leisure lovers, while rich people tend to be consumption lovers. This sort of systematic bias in preferences is clearly inegalitarian since recipients of high wages (a work incentive in itself) also inherit a taste for labor, and recipients of large inherited fortunes receive a taste for work which may overcome the disincentive effects of the unearned wealth.

The simulation procedure here was slightly different from that of Regime II. Since taste parameters (in particular ξ) were not actual data, it was not felt necessary to preserve the same observations. Instead, a new vector of ξ parameters was generated by the linear transformation

$$\xi^* = a\xi + bw_0 + cK_0 + d,$$

where the values of the scalars a, b, c, and d depended on the desired degree of correlation. Since ξ is a normal variate, ξ^* remains approximately normal; and, by judicious choice of the constants, the mean and standard deviation of ξ^* can be made equal to the mean and standard deviation of ξ. This was the technique followed, for a variety of different correlations. For reasons elaborated earlier, it is difficult to make any variate highly correlated with a K_0 vector consisting mainly of zeros. Thus for the moderate correlation case (Regime IIIa) I have chosen $r(\xi, w_0) = -0.37$ and $r(\xi, K_0) = -0.16$. As an example of extremely high correlation of tastes with economic circumstances, I have set $r(\xi, w_0) = -0.77$ and $r(\xi, K_0) = -0.26$ in Regime IIIb. While anecdotal evidence and intuition suggest that negative correlations are the empirically relevant possibility, the effects of positive correlations (of roughly similar magnitude) were also investigated to see if there were any striking asymmetries. Thus Regime IIIc sets $r(\xi, w_0) = +0.38$ and $r(\xi, K_0) = +0.15$; while Regime IIId is defined by $r(\xi, w_0) = +0.73$ and $r(\xi, K_0) = +0.32$. Table 4.6 presents the simulation results for the four variants of the programmed society. These figures may usefully be compared wth the corresponding data in Table 4.5 for the egalitarian society, where tastes are independent.

The most outstanding observation from Table 4.6 is that correlated tastes have a much larger potential impact on inequality than correlated wages.[28] Using the Gini concentration ratio, a moderate amount of programmed taste formation increases inequality by 13%; and an extreme case of correlated tastes increases inequality by over 25%. (Compare line 2 in Tables 4.5 and 4.6.) The coefficient of variation tells an even more dramatic story: inequality rises by almost 20% from Regime I to Regime IIIa, and by more than 40% in going from Regime I to Regime IIIb. (See line 3 in the two tables.)

As before, the explanation for this phenomenon is contained in lines 4–6. It turns out that negative correlation between ξ and w_0 and K_0 is much more potent in destroying the "normal" negative correlation between K_0 and M than is correlation between K_0 and w_0. For example, the positive correlation between K_0 and M in Regime IIIa (moderately correlated tastes) is about the same as the corresponding correlation in Regime IIb (extreme correlation between wages and inheritance). Furthermore, as lines 4 and 5 show, whereas correlated inheritances (Regime II) made the distribution of labor incomes more equal, correlated tastes have the opposite effect. In the programmed society, persons endowed with high wages and/or a large inheritance are also endowed with a taste for labor, resulting in extreme inequality in earnings.

28. Of course, there is no sense in which equal correlation coefficients for Regimes II and IIIa are "equivalent." However, it remains true that even implausibly strong correlation between w_0 and K_0 has a negligible effect upon income inequality, while fairly weak correlation between ξ and w_0 (and K_0) has a substantial impact.

TABLE 4.6 SIMULATION RESULTS FOR THE PROGRAMMED SOCIETY

Characteristic	Regime IIIa	Regime IIIb	Regime IIIc	Regime IIId
(1) $r(\xi, w_0)$	−0.37	−0.77	0.38	0.73
$r(\xi, K_0)$	−0.16	−0.26	0.15	0.32
Inequality of $K_0 + M$				
(2) (a) Gini Ratio	0.333	0.369	0.252	0.206
(3) (b) Coeff. of Variation	0.671	0.802	0.471	0.394
Inequality of M				
(4) (a) Gini Ratio	0.336	0.367	0.259	0.215
(5) (b) Coeff. of Variation	0.633	0.754	0.461	0.379
(6) $r(K_0, M)$	0.034	0.148	−0.221	−0.306
(7) Labor's Share	0.843	0.838	0.847	0.848
(8) Federal Tax Burden	0.257	0.268	0.255	0.254
(9) Average Lifetime Earnings	$121,695	$127,347	$112,009	$107,941
(10) Number of Retirees	51	47	52	50

The unlikely versions of Regime III where tastes are actually an equalizing factor exhibit opposite, and approximately equivalent, tendencies. Lifetime incomes are noticeably equalized when the taste for leisure has positive correlation with the wage and inherited wealth. The reasons are the same. Taste formation makes the distribution of earnings more equal, and also enhances the negative correlation between K_0 and M.

Lines 7–10 of Table 4.6 show that the nondistributional aspects of the economy are not much affected by either the *degree* of endogeneity of tastes, or the *sign* of the correlation. The only substantial effect is on average lifetime earnings, which grow larger when the taste for leisure is negatively correlated with wage rates, and grow smaller when high-productivity persons also are leisure-lovers.

Line 7 suggests a weak negative association between labor's share and the Gini ratio for overall income. It is intuitively clear that this should be the case, since labor's share is reduced by making ξ negatively correlated with w_0. It is enlightening to consider these findings in the light of the frequently heard—and frequently believed!—assertion that equalization of the factor share distribution (that is, an increase in labor's share) has been an important *cause* of equalization in the size distribution.[29] The simulation suggests that both may have been *effects* of some underlying structural change in the economic environment which produced greater equality.

Finally, line 8 suggests that even the strictly proportional tax system entails some minimal progressivity since the overall tax burden rises with inequality. The reason for this is that bequests, which are taxed while consumption is not, are a luxury good.

I conclude that the assumptions on tastes which are employed have a significant impact on the simulated income distribution. The assumption of an extremely programmed society (Regime IIIb) is probably untenable both on a priori grounds and because of its distributional implications. The assumption of moderate correlation of tastes (as in Regime IIIa), however, seems vaguely plausible. The whole notion of "explaining" tastes, unfortunately, leaves one with an uneasy feeling. I certainly would place no great confidence in the hypothesis of negative correlation. For this reason, the investigations to follow will examine the effects of specific parameter changes in economies both with and without correlated tastes.

4.4.4 The Stratified Society (Regime IV)

Of course, an economy might be characterized by both inequality of opportunity and endogenous taste determination as in the programmed society. Indeed, it has been suggested that in the United States unequal educational opportunity makes wages correlated with the economic status of one's parents; while Harrington's hypothesis about the "cycle of poverty" makes leisure-lovers out of poor children. Regime IV is such a *stratified society*.

Four possible instances of the stratified society are considered. Regime IVa, is, roughly, a combination of Regimes IIa and IIIa; that is, $r(w_0, K_0) = +0.26$ and tastes are moderately correlated with endowments. This seems the most plausible version. Regime IVb differs in that tastes become extremely correlated with w_0 and K_0; and Regime IVc modifies Regime IVa by increasing the correlation between K_0 and w_0. The previous results suggest that Regime IVb has a more unequal distribution of income than Regime IVc. Finally, Regime IVd is the most inegalitarian of all the milieus; wages are highly correlated with inherited wealth, while the taste for leisure has a strong negative correlation with both w_0 and K_0. Table 4.7

29. Of the many possible sources I could quote for this view see, for example, Denison [1954], Goldsmith [1957] and Haley [1969]. For an unusual skeptical opinion see Solow [1960, p. 110].

summarizes the simulation results for each of these versions of Regime IV.

In view of the findings for the other regimes, the table contains no real surprises. Using the Gini measure, I have previously found that the presence of moderate correlation between K_0 and w_0 raises inequality of lifetime incomes by about 2% (see Table 4.5, line 2), and moderately correlated tastes raise inequality about 13% (see Table 4.6). In Regime IVa, these two factors jointly raise inequality some 16%. The other three versions also suggest a small positive interaction, that is correlated wages and correlated tastes *together* cause slightly more inequality than the sum of the effects of each taken separately. The coefficient of variation measure corroborates this story. For example, adding moderate correlation between w_0 and K_0 adds 3% to inequality, while adding moderately correlated tastes to Regime I adds about 20%. Both effects acting together (Regime IVa) add some 26%. Similarly, regardless of which measure is used, comparing Regimes IVb and IVc confirms the notion that correlation of tastes with endowments is a more potent disequalizer than correlation of wages with inherited wealth.

TABLE 4.7 SIMULATION RESULTS FOR THE STRATIFIED SOCIETY

Characteristic	Regime IVa	Regime IVb	Regime IVc	Regime IVd
(1) $r(w_0, K_0)$	0.26	0.26	0.51	0.51
$r(\xi, w_0)$	−0.40	−0.80	−0.44	−0.82
$r(\xi, K_0)$	−0.22	−0.35	−0.26	−0.40
Inequality of $K_0 + M$				
(2) (a) Gini Ratio	0.343	0.385	0.354	0.392
(3) (b) Coeff. of Variation	0.709	0.888	0.838	0.968
Inequality of M				
(4) (a) Gini Ratio	0.324	0.368	0.329	0.369
(5) (b) Coeff. of Variation	0.616	0.778	0.672	0.797
(6) $r(K_0, M)$	0.260	0.440	0.638	0.740
(7) Labor's Share	0.842	0.838	0.838	0.835
(8) Federal Tax Burden	0.258	0.260	0.259	0.261
(9) Average Lifetime Earnings	$122,053	$129,169	$123,820	$129,939
(10) Number of Retirees	46	42	44	40

In all versions of Regime IV total income exhibits more inequality than earnings considered alone. This, of course, must be the case when the correlation between earnings and inheritance is positive (see line 6). In fact, the empirical value of this correlation may be a good way to test whether or not the real world corresponds more closely to the egalitarian society or to one of the other regimes. The previously cited study by Projector, Weiss, and Thoresen [1969] suggests that the egalitarian society may not be such a bad approximation after all.

The nondistributional characteristics of the stratified society are not very different from the earlier regimes. In general (and all these tendencies are weak) the more inegalitarian economies have (1) a smaller share for labor in national income, (2) a higher tax burden, (3) higher average earnings, (4) fewer retirees.

In summary, I would offer either Regime I, Regime IIa, or Regime IVa as the closest replica of the contemporary American economy. Deciding whether or not there is inequality of opportunity in the sense used here does not seem terribly important. Deciding whether or not tastes are programmed, however, is vital. Since casual empiricism cannot decide this issue, it will be safest to consider all three regimes as open possibilities.

To give the reader a better idea of the differences among the lifetime income distributions of the three regimes, Table 4.8 presents the distributions by fractiles in Regimes IIa and IVa. These may be compared with Table 4.4 for Regime I. It is apparent that the distributional changes caused by adding correlation between w_0 and K_0 are quite different from the changes that result from adding correlated tastes. In going from Regime I to Regime IIa the changes in fractile shares are minimal. The only notable gain comes in the highest decile, and that appears to be mainly at the expense of the ninth decile. By contrast, in comparing Regime IVa with Regime I the changes are much more dramatic. The lowest 70% of the income distribution loses ground mostly to the upper 10%; the eighth and ninth deciles are affected only minimally. The top 5% and top 1% especially enhance their positions. In other words, the disequalization between Regimes I and IIa amounts to a trivial reshuffling of incomes, while the redistribution in going from Regime I to Regime IVa is clearly from most of the population to the upper echelons.

Finally, in the light of these simulation results, let me briefly examine one of the chief arguments made in favor of income inequality. The rich, it is alleged, have a higher marginal propensity to save.

Therefore, measures which reduce inequality have an unavoidable cost in terms of drying up the supply of savings, and thereby reducing the rate of economic growth.

The reader will recall from Chapter 2 that the plausible allegation that the rich have a higher *lifetime* MPS requires a particular relationship between two taste parameters. In particular, it assumes $\delta > \beta$ so that bequests are a luxury good. I have specifically made this assumption in the simulations: yet the results—compare line 7 in Tables 4.5, 4.6 and 4.7—show little effect of inequality on the supply of loanable funds. The share of property income in total GNP is 16.5% in the most stratified society (Regime IVd) as compared to 15.4% in the egalitarian society—hardly a dramatic change. Further, modern growth theory should make economists suspicious of any argument suggesting that a change in the savings ratio has any *permanent* influence on the economy's growth rate.

TABLE 4.8 INCOME DISTRIBUTION UNDER INEQUALITY OF OPPORTUNITY AND IN THE STRATIFIED SOCIETY

		Inequality of Opportunity Regime IIa	The Stratified Society Regime IVa
Population Group		Share in Total	Share in Total
Lowest	10%	2.76%	2.38%
Second	10%	4.62	4.10
Third	10%	6.00	5.38
Fourth	10%	7.20	6.67
Fifth	10%	8.47	7.90
Sixth	10%	9.69	9.24
Seventh	10%	11.13	10.81
Eighth	10%	12.76	12.71
Ninth	10%	15.42	15.82
Highest	10%	21.95	24.99
Top	5%	12.91	15.35
Top	1%	3.77	4.97

Appendix 4.1 The Question of Sampling Variance

The sample of households created for the simulations reported in this and the following chapters was created by splicing to actual wage and inheritance data three taste parameters—all drawn from Gaussian populations. The perceptive reader might wonder, then, how large the sampling variances of the various statistics might be. That is, a different drawing of 400 triples of taste parameters (or even a different assignment of the same 400 drawings to the 400 wages) would result in a different Gini ratio, and so on. To answer this question twenty-five runs were made for the standard case of the egalitarian society, each time taking different taste parameters. In this way, it is possible to obtain some idea of the sampling variances of the different characteristics (see Table 4.9).

Two points bear mentioning before presenting the results. First, the estimates in the table are not true sampling variances for the whole study since they tacitly assume that a redrawing of 400 wages and inheritances would give exactly the same results. Since the 400 inheritance figures were fabricated to fit a very crude frequency distribution, this is not a very realistic supposition. Secondly, it is *not* true that any changes in the Gini ratio that fall within the bounds of,

TABLE 4.9 SAMPLING STATISTICS

Variable	Mean	Standard Deviation	Highest	Lowest
Gini Ratio of:				
(a) $K_0 + M$	0.296	0.007	0.309	0.285
(b) M	0.302	0.008	0.318	0.291
Correlation between				
K_0 and M	−0.161	0.026	−0.103	−0.194
Average Earnings	$116,512	$1,448	$119,840	$113,972
Number of Retirees	49.6	7.2	62	36
Labor's Share in				
National Income	0.847	0.002	0.850	0.843
Federal Tax Burden	0.255	0.003	0.249	0.258

Source: Based on 25 trial runs, each with 400 households, of the standard case in Regime I.

Note: The reported standard deviations are the square roots of the variances in the sample. Unbiased estimates of the population variances would be about 4% higher.

say, one standard deviation from the mean are pure chance variations. *Every* run reported in this book was done with *exactly the same*
three taste parameters for each of the 400 households. Thus, even a
change in the Gini ratio of 0.001 is "real" (though trivially small) and
not "statistical." At the same time, the sampling variances give some
idea as to what is a "large" effect and what is a "small" effect. That
is, if the total impact of some policy on the Gini coefficient is less
than the chance variation in that coefficient that might result from
drawing a new sample of 400 households from the same population,
it seems safe to conclude that the policy is not a very potent one.

5
The Decomposition of Inequality

...a man...can stare stupidly at phenomena; but in the absence of imagination they will not connect themselves together in any rational way.

C.S. Peirce

As has been stated earlier, the strength of the simulation method lies in its ability to answer the kinds of counterfactual questions that do not admit readily to statistical treatment. How unequal would the income distribution be if inherited wealth were distributed equally? How unequal would it be if everyone had the same taste for leisure?

Now that it has been established that a theoretical model of a perfectly functioning capitalist economy can indeed produce the degree of inequality observed in the real world, it is appropriate to consider the *quantitative* dimensions of the various causes of inequality. Among the more obvious sources of dispersion in incomes, the following seem relevant to all capitalist societies:

1. unequal inherited wealth; or, in fact
2. the existence of inherited wealth at all, even if equal;
3. dispersion in wage rates caused by
(a) unequal abilities
(b) unequal education and training;
4. dispersion in tastes, especially in relative liking of leisure versus consumption goods;
5. unequal rates of return on wealth. Owing to transactions indivisibilities and the advantages of risk pooling through diversification, there are probably considerable increasing returns to wealth-holding by an individual.[1]

1. Evidence for this is provided by Projector, Weiss, and Thoresen [1969, p. 111], who report a Gini ratio for property income of 0.93 for the United States in 1962, as compared to the Gini ratio for net worth of 0.76 reported by Projector and Weiss [1966, p. 30].

And of special relevance to the United States, it seems appropriate to add:

6. racial and sexual discrimination in employment and wages;

7. uneven incidence of unemployment;

8. the effects of monopolies and monopsonies, especially the more powerful trade unions.

The ultimate positive study of the U.S. income distribution would culminate in a breakdown of, say, the total Gini coefficient of lifetime income into that part accounted for by each of these eight causes, and perhaps others. This is a very important question for social policy. The implications for both social stability and the quality of life are very different in an economy where most of the observed inequality is due to differences in tastes, abilities, and stage in the life cycle, as opposed to an economy where most of the inequality is caused by inherited wealth, discrimination, and monopoly power. While this breakdown is terribly important, it is impossible to make empirically. Nature does not provide the econometrician with the controlled experiments he needs. Too many things have changed in the United States since 1900 for time series analysis of income inequality, even were a long enough time series available, to explain the observed movements in inequality.[2] Similar difficulties beset cross-section studies across nations; and this is compounded by the noncomparability of income distribution statistics from different countries.

Simulation, it would appear, is the *only* way this important question can be answered. The present study takes only a few strides towards this goal. The model is quite well equipped to deal with some of the causes of inequality, but not so well equipped for others. For example, it can—as will shortly be shown—determine the disequalizing effects of inherited wealth and dispersion in wages. But it cannot, until a satisfactory model of the education-ability-wages nexus is provided, decompose the effect of wage dispersion into the part due to ability (which, presumably, is "good" or at least tolerable) and the part due to unequal opportunities (which, presumably, is "bad"). The model, as it stands, can cope adequately with the effects of differences in tastes, but has not considered the impact of different rates of return. This factor could conceivably be added, but I have not attempted that here. Turning to those aspects uniquely important to the American economy, by using *actual* observed wage rates, the

2. For a heroic attempt in this direction, see Chiswick and Mincer [1972, pp. S51–S52].

model automatically accounts for *that part of the impact of discrimination and unionization that operates through wage rates*. However, it does not come to grips with the direct effects (if any) of these phenomena on hours of work, and fails completely to consider the incidence of unemployment.[3]

Nevertheless, owing to the extreme importance of the question, it is worth providing even a partial answer. In Section 5.1, therefore, I begin this task by breaking down the observed Gini coefficient of $K_0 + M$ in each regime into the parts attributable to each of the following five causes:

1. the tax system;
2. differences in tastes;
3. the existence of inherited wealth at all;
4. the unequal distribution of inherited wealth;
5. the dispersion in wage rates.

This is done in two different ways. First, starting always from the standard case, I investigate the responses of the Gini coefficient to certain hypothetical changes (for example, an equalization of all tastes). Second, starting from an imaginary economy of identical individuals, I add first one and then another cause of inequality and observe how the Gini ratio "grows."

In Section 5.2 I delve somewhat more deeply into the factor that seems to account for the most inequality—the dispersion in wage rates. Here, since a satisfactory model is yet to be developed, my approach is crudely empirical. Making use of a cross-section study of individual wages, I estimate the effect on overall income inequality of obliterating alternatively black-white, male-female, and union-nonunion wage differentials.

The last section raises a question which is important both in its own right and because it contributes to an assessment of the "goodness of fit" of the entire simulation apparatus. For the first time in the book a population of people of all ages—rather than an age cohort—is considered, and the distribution of *annual*—rather than lifetime—income is simulated. The results turn out to be remarkably close to the actual American income distribution and enable me to estimate the fraction of the inequality observed in U.S. data which is simply attributable to people being at different stages in their life cycles.

---

3. On the latter, see Solow [1951].

5.1 The Causes of Inequality in Lifetime Incomes

5.1.1 The Egalitarian Society (Regime I)

Table 5.1 indicates the impact on the Gini coefficient for $K_0 + M$ of each of several hypothetical changes in the economic environment of the egalitarian society. In each case, I have simulated the standard case of subsection 4.4.1 with only one modification. In line 1, both tax rates are set to zero. In lines 2–4 the variance of each taste parameter is, in turn, set to zero while the mean remains the same. Line 5 combines lines 2–4 by giving all individuals identical tastes. Line 6 alters the distribution of inherited wealth by giving each family the mean inheritance, $5,754; and line 7 takes the more radical step of equalizing all inherited wealth at zero. Finally, line 8 shows the effect of a hypothetical equalization of all wage rates.

The results in Table 5.1 point overwhelmingly in one direction, suggesting that equalizing the distribution of wages is the only way to effect a substantial redistribution of income. The proportional tax system, as one would expect, has almost no effect on inequality. (The potential effects of certain explicitly redistributive tax systems will be considered in the next chapter.) Of the three taste parameters, only ξ, the taste for leisure versus consumption, seems to have any significant effect on inequality. Considering the extreme dispersion given to the parameter b,[4] it is rather surprising that it contributes so little to

TABLE 5.1 IMPACTS ON GINI RATIO IN THE EGALITARIAN SOCIETY

Change from Standard Case	Effect on Gini Ratio		
(1) Remove proportional taxes	-0.000		
(2) Equalize labor-leisure tastes (ξ)	-0.024	or	-8.3%
(3) Equalize taste for bequests (b)	-0.001	or	-0.2%
(4) Equalize time preferences (ρ)	$+0.000$	or	$+0.1\%$
(5) Equalize all tastes	-0.026	or	-8.7%
(6) Equalize inheritances at $5,754	-0.010	or	-3.5%
(7) Equalize inheritances at zero	-0.006	or	-2.0%
(8) Equalize wage rates	-0.161	or	-54.6%

Note: A change of "$+0.000$" means an increase in the Gini ratio of less than 0.0005. Conversely, a change of "-0.000" means a decrease in the Gini ratio of less than -0.0005.

4. The reader will recall that $E(b) = \sigma(b) = 0.25$.

inequality. Chance variations in ρ, in fact, have a negligible *equalizing* effect. It should be noted however, that equalization of ξ has more impact when ρ and b are also equalized (compare lines 2 and 5).

Lines 6 and 7 contain the most startling information of all. Line 6, for example, simulates a quite radical reform of the inheritance laws whereby all bequests would be confiscated by the government and redistributed equally among all consumer units. Yet it appears that even such an extremely egalitarian policy would improve the Gini ratio by only 3.5%. Line 7 points out that if, instead of redistributing the bequests in equal amounts, the government merely commandeered all estates (this is *not* a balanced-budget policy), the equalizing effects would be cut almost in half. Because of the work disincentive provided by inheritance, it appears that, once a policy of equal inheritance for all has been decided upon, a large inheritance level is preferable to a zero level.[5] The reader should realize that this conclusion—that a radical reform of inheritance policies can accomplish comparatively little income redistribution—has been reached starting from an extremely unequal distribution of K_0. The Gini ratio of K_0 is 0.938; the top 1% of households receives almost 55% of all inherited wealth while the bottom 80% receives less than 1%. Yet even a completely equal division of this inheritance pool would lower the Gini ratio of lifetime incomes by only 0.01.

Of course, it can still be objected that such a conclusion might not stand up in a model which included some truly fabulous fortunes, that is, if J. Paul Getty were included in the sample of 400 persons. This is a difficult question to answer since the expected number of, say, million-dollar inheritances in a sample of 400 is zero. For example, according to federal estate tax returns—and this already covers only about the top 2.5% of all estates[6]—only 3.3% of the returns filed in 1969 were for gross estates over $1 million.[7] Based on this one might hazard the guess that about 0.083% (2.5% $\times$ 3.3%) of all estates exceeded $1 million, that is, about one in 1,200. So a much larger sample size is needed to replicate adequately the extreme upper tail of the inheritance distribution.

As a weak test of the importance of giant fortunes, I resimulated the standard case of the egalitarian society with the highest inheritance raised from $479,000 to $4,790,000. Note that this certainly

5. This assumes that the goal is to minimize inequality. Another goal, for example, to maximize aggregate labor supply, would lead to a very different optimal inheritance level.
6. According to R.J. Lampman [1962, p. 11].
7. U.S. Internal Revenue Service [1972, Table 8, p. 20].

gives an overestimate of the importance of large fortunes. The resulting distribution of K_0 is absurdly unequal: the Gini ratio is 0.962, and 1/4 of 1% of the population receives 72 1/2% of all inherited wealth. A further indication is that the sample correlation between K_0 and $K_0 + M$ rises to a phenomenal $+0.965$, implying that a simple regression of lifetime incomes on inherited wealth in this economy would explain 93% of the variance of the former. Surely no modern economy has ever been so inegalitarian as this. The result of the stimulation is that the Gini ratio rises dramatically to 0.350. Comparing this with previous outcomes suggests that abolition of inheritance in such a regime would lower the Gini ratio by a substantial 0.055. This, in turn, suggests that experimentation with a much larger synthetic sample including some very large fortunes might be worthwhile.

Finally, line 8 reveals the one place the state may have real leverage if it desires to affect the income distribution. Something like 55% of all the observed inequality appears to be caused by unequal wage rates. This suggests that one way to achieve an equalization of income may be through some sort of wage subsidy program—an idea that is tested in the following chapter.

Table 5.2 considers the same set of questions from the opposite point of view; that is, instead of *decomposing* the inequality I *build it up* from zero. In the hypothetical world upon which most economic theory is based, where all individuals have the same tastes, same inheritance, and same wage rates, there would be no inequality of

TABLE 5.2 DERIVATION OF THE GINI
RATIO IN THE EGALITARIAN SOCIETY

Type of Economy	Gini Ratio
All persons identical	0.000
Different tastes No inheritances Equal wages	0.121
Different tastes Actual K_0 distribution Equal wages	0.134
Standard case	0.295

incomes. Adding to this world dispersion in tastes (as in the standard case), results in a Gini ratio of 0.121 which is about 41% of the total inequality. If, keeping wages the same, I then superimpose the actual American distribution of inherited wealth, the Gini ratio rises to only 0.134, an additional 4.4% of the ultimate total. This corroborates the relatively small role assigned to inheritance by Table 5.1, and leaves almost 55% to be accounted for by wage dispersion.[8]

One might tentatively conclude for the egalitarian society that, in round numbers—

1. about 40% of the observed lifetime inequality is due to differences in tastes, and thus "desirable." However, with the other inequalities already present, equalization of tastes would decrease overall inequality by less than 10%.

2. about 4 to 5% of observed inequality is caused by unequal inheritances.

3. about 55% of the inequality is directly attributable to differences in wage rates. I defer to the next section the question of how much of this 55% can be attributed to race and sex discrimination or to unionism, and how much is left to other factors (like genetic and acquired ability).

5.1.2 The Other Regimes

With the method by now clear, I shall quickly review the simulation results for the other regimes. Tables 5.3 and 5.4 contain the same information as Tables 5.1 and 5.2 for the two possible versions of inequality of opportunity (Regime II). Basically, they corroborate the ideas obtained from the previous tables. Again, disparities in wages dominate all other causes of inequality. With moderate correlation between w_0 and K_0 (Regime IIa) equalization of tastes is a somewhat stronger equalizing factor than it was in Regime I; but with very high correlation tastes have about the same impact as they did there. Line 1 strongly suggests that removal of the two taxes would cause a slight increase in inequality. The reason is the previously cited high income elasticity of bequests, which lends some mild progressivity to even a proportional estate tax.

Tables 5.5 and 5.6 repeat this same information for the four possible versions of the programmed society (Regime III). The reader

8. Due to interaction effects, the derivation of the Gini ratio presented in Table 5.2, as well as in Tables 5.4, 5.6 and 5.8 to follow, is somewhat sensitive to the *order* in which the various causes of inequality are added. Rather than bore the reader with every possible permutation, I have settled upon one particular order selected to reflect declining degrees of exogeneity (from tastes to inheritances to wages).

TABLE 5.3 IMPACTS ON GINI RATIO UNDER INEQUALITY OF
OPPORTUNITY

Change from Standard Case	Effects on Gini Ratio in	
	Regime IIa	Regime IIb
(1) Remove proportional taxes	+0.001	+0.002
(2) Equalize labor-leisure tastes	−0.026	−0.023
(3) Equalize taste for bequests	−0.001	−0.001
(4) Equalize time preferences	+0.000	−0.000
(5) Equalize all tastes	−0.028	−0.025
(6) Equalize inheritances at $5,754	−0.016[a]	−0.015[a]
(7) Equalize inheritances at zero	−0.011[a]	−0.011[a]
(8) Equalize wage rates	−0.166	−0.168

[a]This case is indistinguishable from Regime I.

TABLE 5.4 DERIVATION OF THE GINI RATIO UNDER
INEQUALITY OF OPPORTUNITY

Type of Economy	Gini Ratio in	
	Regime IIa	Regime IIb
All persons identical	0.000	0.000
Different tastes	0.121[a]	0.121[a]
Unequal inheritance	0.134	0.132
Unequal wage rates	0.300	0.300

[a]This case is indistinguishable from Regime I.

will recall that IIIa signifies moderate negative correlation between ξ and w_0 and K_0; IIIb represents strong negative correlation; and IIIc and IIId capture the effects of unlikely positive correlations. The results reported in these tables are about as expected. Once again, dispersion in wages dominates all other causes. Inequality in wages causes more inequality in income when the taste for leisure is negatively correlated wth wages, and less inequality when the taste for leisure is positively correlated. Similarly, equalizing tastes would be a far stronger egalitarian change in Regimes IIIa and IIIb (as compared to Regime I), but would of course be disequalizing in Regimes IIIc and IIId. Using Table 5.5 and 5.6 to break down the causes of inequality in Regime IIIa as I did for Regime I, I might hazard the guess that —
1. 36% (0.120) is due to taste dispersion; but with interactions present a complete equalization of tastes would reduce inequality only about 19%;
2. 4% (0.015) is due to inheritance;
3. 48% (0.061) is due to wage dispersion;
4. 12% (0.037) is due to correlation of tastes with wages and inheritance.

Finally, Tables 5.7 and 5.8 report the same information for the stratified society, the regimes that combine positive correlation between w_0 and K_0 with negative correlation between ξ and endowments. The same general picture emerges. Wage dispersion is far and away the most important single cause of inequality, though in regimes where the correlation between endowments and ξ is extreme differences in tastes are also quite significant. The proportional tax system now turns out to be a slight disequalizer[9] (though never by very much); and equal inheritances are considerably better than no inheritances at all. Using Regime IVa as the most plausible version, and continuing my heroic "guesstimates," I might surmise that inequality is caused—
1. 35% (0.121) by differences in tastes;
2. 5% (0.018) by unequal inherited wealth;
3. 47% (0.161) by dispersion in wage rates;
4. 13% (0.042) by the intercorrelations among K_0, w_0, and ξ.

In retrospect, the four most plausible regimes (I, IIa, IIIa, IVa) agree rather more closely than might have been expected. All point to

9. The reason, I suppose, is that income taxation reduces M proportionately for each family, but does not affect K_0. Thus it appears slightly disequalizing. Of course, including the effect of the inheritance tax on K_0 might upset this conclusion.

TABLE 5.5 IMPACTS ON GINI RATIO IN THE PROGRAMMED SOCIETY

Change from Standard Case	Effects on Gini Ratio under Regime—			
	IIIa	IIIb	IIIc	IIId
(1) Remove proportional taxes	− 0.001	− 0.002	+ 0.001	+ 0.004
(2) Equalize labor-leisure tastes	− 0.063[a]	− 0.099[a]	+ 0.018[a]	+ 0.064[a]
(3) Equalize taste for bequests	− 0.001	− 0.001	− 0.001	− 0.001
(4) Equalize time preferences	+ 0.001	+ 0.001	+ 0.001	+ 0.000
(5) Equalize all tastes	− 0.064[a]	− 0.100[a]	+ 0.017[a]	+ 0.063[a]
(6) Equalize inheritances at $5,754	− 0.011	− 0.013	− 0.010	− 0.012
(7) Equalize inheritances at zero	− 0.007	− 0.009	− 0.006	− 0.007
(8) Equalize wage rates	− 0.198	− 0.228	− 0.122	− 0.083

[a]This case is indistinguishable from Regime I.

TABLE 5.6 DERIVATION OF GINI RATIO IN THE PROGRAMMED SOCIETY

Type of Economy	Gini Ratio in Regime—			
	IIIa	IIIb	IIIc	IIId
All persons identical	0.000	0.000	0.000	0.000
Different tastes	0.120	0.122	0.120	0.114
Unequal inheritances	0.135	0.142	0.131	0.124
Unequal wage rates	0.333	0.369	0.252	0.206

the relative unimportance of inherited wealth in the overall picture, attribute around 40% of total inequality to differing tastes, and underscore the overriding importance of unequal wages.

5.2 Wage Dispersion and Income Inequality

As indicated earlier, I do not believe that a satisfactory model of wage dispersion has as yet been devised. In view of the results just obtained, this leaves size distribution theory in a rather awkward position, not unlike the proverbial *Hamlet* without the Prince of Denmark. Of course, I have not written the Prince out of the play; he simply has yet to make his appearance.

Until a rigorous model of the inequality in wage rates is developed, one can either close the story with the simple statement that the (unexplained) wage distribution is the primary determinant of the income distribution; or one can attempt to make some crude empiri-

TABLE 5.7 IMPACTS ON GINI RATIO IN THE STRATIFIED SOCIETY

Change from Standard Case	Effect on Gini Ratio under Regime			
	IVa	IVb	IVc	IVd
(1) Remove proportional taxes	−0.000	−0.002	−0.001	−0.002
(2) Equalize labor-leisure tastes	−0.068[a]	−0.111[a]	−0.078[b]	−0.116[b]
(3) Equalize taste for bequests	−0.001	−0.001	−0.001	−0.001
(4) Equalize time preferences	+0.001	+0.001	+0.001	+0.001
(5) Equalize all tastes	−0.070[a]	−0.113[a]	−0.079[b]	−0.117[a]
(6) Equalize inheritances at $5,754	−0.017	−0.020	−0.021	−0.023
(7) Equalize inheritances at zero	−0.013	−0.015	−0.016	−0.019
(8) Equalize wage rates	−0.203	−0.234	−0.210	−0.237

[a]This case is indistinguishable from Regime IIa.
[b]This case is indistinguishable from Regime IIb.

TABLE 5.8 DERIVATION OF GINI RATIO IN THE STRATIFIED SOCIETY

Type of Economy	Gini Ratio under Regime—			
	IVa	IVb	IVc	IVd
All persons identical	0.000	0.000	0.000	0.000
Different tastes	0.121	0.126	0.123	0.127
Unequal inheritances	0.139	0.151	0.144	0.155
Unequal wage rates	0.342	0.385	0.354	0.392

cal guesses regarding one or the other of the many causes of wage inequality. The present section follows the second course.

5.2.1 The Method

Specifically, I seek to develop estimates of the *quantitative* importance for income inequality of the following three phenomena: discrimination against blacks, discrimination against females, and union-nonunion wage differentials. The method of inquiry is as follows. In some previous empirical work [Blinder, 1971, 1973a], I have developed regression equations to explain individual wage rates on the basis of socioeconomic characteristics. More precisely, I have estimated regressions of the form

$$\log w_i = \alpha \cdot X_i + \beta_1 R_i + \beta_2 S_i + \beta_3 U_i + e_i, \tag{5.1}$$

where w_i is the wage rate of individual i, X_i is a vector of characteristics of the individual which are being controlled for, R_i (race) is a dummy variable equal to unity for blacks and zero for whites, S_i (sex) is a dummy equal to one for males and zero for females, U_i (union) is a dummy equal to unity for union members and zero for nonmembers, the vector α and the scalars β_1, β_2, β_3 are constants, and e_i is a stochastic error. Under this specification, for example, β_1 can be interpreted as the *percentage* reduction in wages attributable to being black, all other things held equal.

Such a regression enables me to correct for the pure effect of black skin, or female gender, or lack of a union card on wage rates in one of two ways. Taking union differentials as an example, I can either multiply all nonunion wage rates by a factor $1 + \beta_3$ to put them on a par with union wages; or I can divide all the union wages by $1 + \beta_3$. What I would like to know, of course, is what the wage distribution *would look like* in the absence of unions. The first procedure essentially assumes that current union wages would remain the same and all nonunion wages would rise by $100\beta_3\%$ if the unions were to disappear all at once. The second procedure adopts the opposing extreme assumption; namely that union wages would fall by $100\beta_3\%$ while nonunion wages would be unaffected. Presumably, the actual effect of the abolition of unions would be somewhere in between these two extremes; union wages would fall somewhat and nonunion wages would rise. So looking at the effect on the income distribution in both ways supplies bounds on the true effect of unionism on income distribution. If these bounds are rather tight, as they typically turn out to be, the procedures will at least have given an unambiguous estimate of the effect of the unions.

In applying this method to estimate the effects of race, sex, and union membership on wages, a question of obvious importance is, What variables shall be controlled for? That is, what variables belong in the vector X_i? For example, in isolating the effect of racial discrimination on wages, should one control for education and occupation? Surely a black and a white with different educational credentials will earn different wages even in the absence of discrimination. This argues that education, occupation, and the like should be controlled for. But it is equally clear historically that some of the discrimination against blacks has taken the form of denial of access to education and/or relegation to inferior occupations. And this argues against controlling for education and occupation.

In Blinder [1971, 1973a] I argued that it is important to distinguish between *structural* and *reduced-form* wage equations. If one believes, as I do, that education and occupation have a *direct* impact on wage rates, then they should appear in the vector X_i in the structural equation. By contrast, certain other variables which may affect wages only *indirectly*—for example, family background, which may influence schooling and other things but which presumably has no direct effect on wages—ought to be excluded from X_i in the structure. The reduced-form wage equation, of course, would include all variables that influence wage rates either directly or indirectly *and that are exogenous to the individual*. Thus, such obvious determinants of wages as education, occupation, and union membership ought not to appear in the reduced form, while variables like family background should. Thus, in the papers just cited, I estimated both structural and reduced-form wage equations. For present purposes, equation (5.1) adequately represents the structure, while the reduced form is

$$\log w_i = a \cdot Z_i + b_1 R_i + b_2 S_i + v_i, \tag{5.2}$$

where Z_i is some vector different from (though partially overlapping with) X_i, and v_i is a stochastic error. Note that union membership, an endogenous variable in my formulation, appears only in the structural equation; so I have only one estimate of the union impact on wages. However, since race and sex presumably influence wages both directly and indirectly (via educational attainment and the like), (5.1) and (5.2) each provide a separate estimate of the extent of race and sex discrimination. For example, β_1 is an estimate of the direct discrimination against blacks in wages, while b_1 includes also the monetary equivalent of discrimination in education, occupational assignments and union membership.

5.2.2 The Effect of Racial Discrimination on Inequality

Consider first the results on the race differential obtained from the structure. The point estimate of β_1 is -0.223 (with standard error 0.028),[10] indicating that, other things equal, black wages average only 77.7% of those of whites. Therefore, to simulate the end of *direct discrimination in wages only*, I first multiply the wage of every white person in the sample[11] by 0.777 in order to obliterate the race differential. The result[12] is a decline in the Gini ratio of income

10. The empirical estimates cited here and below are from Blinder [1971].
11. As the wages are actual data drawn from the Survey Research Center [1970] data, the race, sex, and union affiliation of each individual are known.
12. All experiments reported in this section were performed using the standard case of the egalitarian society (Regime I).

$(K_0 + M)$ from 0.295 to 0.286. The alternative procedure is to divide every black wage by 0.777, and this leads to a Gini ratio of 0.283.

The two estimates agree quite well, and suggest that racial discrimination, while indubitably an urgent social problem on other grounds, is simply not a major contributor to inequality in the overall income distribution. To me, at least, this is an unexpected finding, but the explanation is not hard to find. It is well known that there is substantial inequality between the races; but those familiar with American income distribution statistics also know that the inequality *among blacks* is far greater than the inequality *among whites*. This is evidenced in my sample of 400 individuals by Gini ratios for lifetime income of 0.255 within the subset of 282 whites and 0.343 among the 118 blacks. So obliterating the racial wage differential does two things to the overall distribution. Eliminating racial inequality clearly has an equalizing effect. But increasing the fraction of total income going to blacks puts more weight on the group with the more dispersed income distribution, and this is clearly disequalizing. The net result of these two factors is the trivial equalization uncovered by the simulations.

Of course, overt wage discrimination has not been the only obstacle in the way of economic progress for blacks. The coefficient b_1 of race in the reduced form equation is -0.353 (with standard error 0.032), suggesting that when discrimination in education, occupational attainment, and union membership are included the average black earns only 64.7% as much as the average white. When all white wages are multiplied by 0.647, the simulated Gini ratio for income falls to 0.288; and when black wages are divided by 0.647, the resulting concentration ratio is 0.282. Again the two procedures lead to roughly the same conclusion—that eliminating racial discrimination entirely would not make the U.S. income distribution very much more equal.[13]

5.2.3 The Effect of Sex Discrimination on Inequality

The procedure used to assess the significance of sex discrimination as a determinant of income inequality is identical. In the structural equation, the point estimate of β_2 is 0.339 (with standard error 0.031). This means that, holding education, occupation, and many other things equal, males on average earn 33.9% more than females. To simulate the effect of eliminating sex discrimination in wages, then,

13. It would, of course, eradicate the close asociation between skin color and position in the income distribution, a goal that is highly desirable in its own right.

the wage rates of all females are increased by 33.9%. The Gini ratio
for lifetime incomes in this experiment falls to 0.293, an almost
imperceptible drop from the 0.295 when there is sex discrimination.
Adopting the alternative of reducing all male wages by 33.9% leads to
a concentration ratio of 0.297, which is actually higher than in the
absence of discrimination. The conclusion appears to be that sex
discrimination does not lead to any noticeable increase in inequality
in the overall income distribution. The reason is the same as in the
case of blacks. While obliterating the sex differential in wages is
equalizing, placing more weight on the more unequal female income
distribution is disequalizing.[14]

Use of the reduced form coefficient b_3 suggests that raising the
wage of the average female up to the level of the average male would
actually make the overall income distribution more unequal. The
point estimate of b_3 is 0.462 (with standard error 0.031), and when all
female wages are increased 46.2%, the Gini ratio rises to 0.297. When,
instead, all male wages are reduced 46.2%, the corresponding ratio is
0.302. As should be clear by now, the reason for this unexpected
result is the increased weight that is attached to the more unequal
female distribution.

5.2.4 The Effect of Unions on Inequality
As explained in subsection 5.2.1 above, the dummy variable for
union membership appears only in the structure, and therefore I have
just one estimate of the union-nonunion wage differential. In equation (5.1), the point estimate of β_3 is 0.292 (with standard error
0.026). Using this to raise average nonunion wages to equality with
union rates results in a decline in the Gini ratio for lifetime income to
0.280, suggesting a moderate equalization. However, when I reduce
union wages 29.2% instead, the concentration ratio falls only to 0.290,
a negligible decline from the 0.295 of the standard case. The explanation for the small equalization is what we have by now come to
expect: nonunion workers have a much more disperse income disri-
bution than union workers.[15] The large difference between the two
procedures is due, I suppose, to the fact that inheritances (which are
highly unequally distributed) bulk comparatively larger in the simulation in which union wages are reduced.

14. In the sample, the concentration ratio among the 276 men is 0.274, while among
the 134 women it is 0.329.
15. The concentration ratios in the sample are 0.212 for the 134 union members and
0.323 for the 266 nonmembers.

One important caveat should be entered as an epilogue to the results on discrimination and unions just mentioned. In each case I conduct a thought experiment whereby race or sex or union wage differentials are eliminated by magic. Nothing is said about how this program might be effected, and, indeed, I have no intention of discussing such weighty issues here. It is clear, however, that *some* mechanism for eliminating the average race or sex or union pay differential—other than waving a magic wand—would have to be devised. And it would be a strange coincidence indeed if *every* black or female or non-union member benefited by precisely the same percentage. Social policies that, for example, concentrate the gains from ending racial discrimination in the lower tail of the black income distribution would *both* eradicate racial differences *and* equalize the distribution among blacks. It is quite conceivable that such policies might have far more substantial impacts on overall income inequality than has been indicated here. What is suggested is that their equalizing effects would not be much stronger than those of a program to aid families in the lower tail of the *white* distribution.

5.3 The Distribution of Annual Income

I turn now to a question raised several times during the course of this book but as yet unanswered. In the preceding sections of this chapter, I have tentatively attributed the total inequality in *lifetime* incomes to its various causes. However, the observed income distribution is generally for a far shorter accounting period, typically one year. When considering such a distribution, there is an additional cause of dispersion which does not appear in lifetime distributions: the fact that different households are at different stages in their life cycles. Some young households which will ultimately be among the rich in lifetime income appear poor, since the breadwinner is just starting his career (or, perhaps, is still in school). Other older households, which have not adequately provided for their retirement years, have an income standard far below their lifetime average. Also, owing to the two qualitatively different life cycles in leisure and labor outlined in Chapter 3 (increasing leisure versus decreasing leisure), even people of the same age, same labor-leisure tastes, and same endowments may have different incomes if their rates of subjective time discounting are different.

So in order to test the realism of the simulation model—and in particular to discover which regime most closely resembles the U.S.

economy— it is necessary to consider the distribution of annual income in a population composed of diverse age cohorts.

The model of microeconomic behavior developed in Chapters 2 and 3 is quite capable of generating an individual's income at a particular age. So, it would appear, all that is necessary is to superimpose an age distribution for the population and grind out a simulated income distribution. In fact, a few adjustments in the data are also required.

Consider first the age distribution. I was fortunate to have access to the aforementioned Survey Research Center (SRC) tape of 4,460 families which includes, among other things, both the wage rates and ages of the household heads. Since it was felt that a much larger sample was required to simulate a continuous distribution of people of varying ages (whereas only 400 sufficed for a single age cohort), all families on the tape with heads at least 18 years of age (the assumed age of economic birth) and younger than 73 (the assumed age of death) were included in the sample. There were 3,612 such households, and this was arbitrarily truncated to 3,600 for convenience. For each household, the "age" was defined as the actual age of the head minus 18 years. Thus the age variable ran from zero to 54, and reproduced exactly the age distribution in the SRC sample.

The relevant wage variable for each household was not similarly observable since the variable of interest in the theoretical model is *not* the current wage but rather w_0, the wage at economic age zero. In view of the assumption of a constant rate of growth of wage rates m, each current wage rate $w(A)$, where A is the economic age of the individual, was transformed into a hypothetical initial wage rate by the relation $w_0 = e^{-mA} w(A)$. After this alteration, the 3,600 wage observations were entered as the w_0 distribution for the simulation.

The distribution of inherited wealth represented a real problem. On the supposition that the present distribution of inherited wealth is a steady state—an assumption made for lack of contradicting data[16]— the distribution of K_0 used in the sample of 400 was employed again. That is, there were assumed to be nine individuals inheriting each of the K_0 values used in the sample of 400. Since there is a background rate of growth of wealth in the economy, this may introduce some systematic errors (making older people appear richer than they actually are); but it was thought that such errors were not likely to be serious.

16. For what it is worth, Robert Gallman [1969] has constructed an estimate of the wealth distribution in the United States in 1860 which is not too different from the wealth distribution in 1960.

Finally, a distribution of taste parameters—that is, a triple (ξ, b, ρ)—was generated from independent normal distributions as explained in subsection 4.1.3. Since the annual sample of 3,600 is so much larger than the lifetime sample of 400, it was thought that sampling variances would be small enough to be ignored. Owing to the high computational cost of dealing with such a large sample, no runs were made to estimate these sampling variances.

Table 5.9 presents the simulated income distribution for the standard case in the egalitarian society. The estimated Gini coefficient for this distribution is 0.425; the coefficient of variation is 0.941. Average income per household (after tax) is $5,644; the largest is $54,303 while the smallest is −$1,876. This distribution has an uncanny resemblance to actual published data on the U.S. income distribution during the 1960s.

There is some ambiguity as to which factual distribution this simulated distribution should be compared with. Though another

TABLE 5.9 SIMULATED DISTRIBUTION OF ANNUAL INCOME: THE
EGALITARIAN SOCIETY

Population Group	Approximate Income Range	Relative Share
Lowest 10%	$ −1,900 – $ 1,400	1.52%
Second 10%	1,400 – 2,100	3.12
Third 10%	2,100 – 2,700	4.27
Fourth 10%	2,700 – 3,500	5.48
Fifth 10%	3,500 – 4,300	6.83
Sixth 10%	4,300 – 5,200	8.35
Seventh 10%	5,200 – 6,400	10.27
Eighth 10%	6,400 – 8,100	12.71
Ninth 10%	8,100 – 11,000	16.54
Highest 10%	11,000 – 54,300	30.93
Top 5%	14,400 – 54,300	19.98
Top 1%	27,000 – 54,300	6.70
Gini concentration ratio		0.425
Coefficient of variation		0.941

investigator might make a different choice, it seems to me that
distributions over households, or spending units, or some such concept offer the most relevant comparisons. Table 5.10 summarizes
some actual U.S. income distributions which appear conceptually
comparable to the simulation results. (The source for each distribution is explained in the notes to the table.) Though they refer to
different years and slightly diifferent concepts of income and of the
recipient unit, the distributions are reasonably similar to one another.
Comparing these authentic data with the simulated distribution in
Table 5.9 reveals an astonishing similarity. The three annual distributions (columns 1–3 of Table 5.10) have nearly the same Gini ratio as
the simulated distribution.[17] Among the averages of annual distributions (included to average out year-to-year fluctuations in the data
and, hopefully, reduce sampling variation), the CPS data (column 4)
exhibit very slightly less inequality than the simulated data; the latter
seem to assign too much income to the upper and lower tails.
Comparing the simulation to the average OBE distribution (column
5), I would again appear to slightly overestimate inequality, though
the shares of particular fractiles match extraordinarily well; only for
the ninth decile and the upper 1% are the errors substantial.

As the reader by now has probably come to expect, the distribution of annual incomes in Regime IIa[18] does not differ very much
from Regime I, while the distribution under Regime IVa[19] is notably
less equal. These two distributions are given in Table 5.11. The
figures for Regime IVa confirm the previous impression that such a
regime is more inegalitarian than the U.S. economy has been for a
long while.

5.4 Recapitulation

Appending these last results to the previous breakdown of the overall
Gini coefficient for lifetime incomes, and using Regimes I and IIa as
the paradigm cases, I am led to the following (very approximate)
attribution of the total observed inequality (a Gini ratio of 0.43) in
annual incomes.

1. About 30% (or 0.13) of the Gini ratio appears to be caused by

17. Budd's Gini ratios are calculated by a different method. See his paper.
18. The actual correlation between w_0 and K_0 in the annual simulation is 0.24 as
opposed to 0.26 in the lifetime distribution.
19. The actual correlation of ξ with w_0 is -0.41, and with K_0 is -0.21 in the annual
experiment, as compared to -0.40 and -0.22, respectively, in the lifetime experiments.

TABLE 5.10 SOME ACTUAL U.S. INCOME DISTRIBUTIONS

Population Group		(1)	(2)	(3)	(4)	(5)
Lowest	10%	0.94%	1.34%	1%	0.81%	1.39%
Second	10%	2.72	3.22	3	2.63	3.32
Third	10%	4.43	4.77	4	4.37	4.87
Fourth	10%	6.10	6.12	6	6.14	6.20
Fifth	10%	7.76	7.43	7	7.80	7.45
Sixth	10%	9.48	8.80	9	9.54	8.75
Seventh	10%	11.29	10.39	11	11.34	10.26
Eighth	10%	13.37	12.34	13	13.45	12.10
Ninth	10%	16.20	15.53	16	16.35	15.11
Highest	10%	27.72	30.17	30	27.61	30.93
Top	5%	17.50	19.80	20	17.34	20.44
Top	1%	6.01	7.50	NA	5.89	8.04
Gini Ratio		0.416	0.417	0.43	0.418	0.415

Notes:

NA: not available

(1): 1967 Current Population Survey (CPS) distribution for families and unrelated individuals (pooled), as computed by Budd [1970, Table 4, p. 253].

(2): 1961 Office of Business Economics (OBE) distribution for families and unattached individuals (pooled), from Budd [1970, Table 4, p. 253].

(3): 1963 Survey of Financial Characteristics of Consumers (Federal Reserve) distribution for consumer units, as reported by Projector, Weiss and Thoresen [1969, Table 4, p. 128].

(4): Average of nine annual distributions, 1960–68, CPS families and unrelated individuals (pooled), computed from Budd [1970, Table 4, p. 253].

(5): Average of five distributions: 1947, 1950, 1955, 1960, 1961, OBE families and unattached individuals, computed from Budd [1970, Table 4, p. 253].

TABLE 5.11 SIMULATED DISTRIBUTION OF ANNUAL
INCOME: REGIMES IIa AND IVa

Population Group		Share in Regime IIa	Share in Regime IVa
Lowest	10%	1.41%	1.15%
Second	10%	3.20	2.57
Third	10%	4.30	3.49
Fourth	10%	5.38	4.41
Fifth	10%	6.67	5.54
Sixth	10%	8.19	6.84
Seventh	10%	9.94	8.46
Eighth	10%	12.36	10.65
Ninth	10%	16.11	14.18
Highest	10%	32.46	42.72
Top	5%	21.74	32.79
Top	1%	8.21	18.20
Gini concentration ratio		0.436	0.523
Coefficient of variation		1.064	2.366

life-cycle influences, and disappears when the lifetime is taken as the unit of account.

2. About 28% (or 0.12) is due to differences in tastes. This part, of course, is highly conjectural since I have no idea if the constructed distributions of taste parameters are either too disperse or too concentrated. Like the portion attributable to the life cycle, this part of observed inequality is not only tolerable, but actually desirable in a society that prides itself in respecting individual preferences.

3. Only about 2% (or 0.01) is attributable to the unequal distribution of inherited wealth. Presumably none of this would be tolerated in a strictly egalitarian society. But it appears that even radical reforms of current inheritance procedures would not alter the basic inequality of incomes very dramatically.

4. Almost 40% (or 0.17) is attributable to the distribution of wage rates, including any correlation wages might have with inherited

wealth. This is the area that seems to be pinpointed for further research.

There are a number of distinct reasons why wages differ; and the attribution of the total dispersion in wages among these causes has great bearing on social policies towards redistribution. Among the more important causes are—

a. innate ability of individuals, which is transmitted genetically by the parents. Presumably only the most radical of redistributionists would want to eliminate this cause of wage dispersion.

b. unequal educational attainment. This, in turn, may result from differing abilities, inequality of opportunity, and differences in tastes. To the extent that the first and/or the last prevail, one may be quite satisfied with the resulting inequality. However if, as some previous studies indicate, unequal opportunity is at the root of the inequality in educational attainment, the policy prescription is clear.

c. discrimination in wage rates. The distribution of wages fed into the model included wages of blacks and whites, and of males and females. While the simulations suggested that very little of the total dispersion is attributable to race and sex discrimination, further studies are necessary to either buttress or overturn this conclusion. Again, this is presumably one source of inequality which is not tolerable in a society such as ours.

d. unions and other departures from competitive labor market conditions. The question of unions is a vexing one. According to the folklore, if there is at least some monopsony power, unionization shifts distributive shares in favor of labor and against capital, and this should be equalizing. At the same time, unions tend to drive the wages of highly paid hourly employees up closer to parity with salaried workers (which is equalizing), while forcing down the wages received by the lower paid sectors of the labor force (which is disequalizing). A consensus—supported by no facts that I know of—seems to have evolved around the point of view that "...the direct effect of unionism upon the distribution of personal incomes is...minor."[20] Of course, this is a consensus based on casual empiricism, and therefore not terribly persuasive. My simulations really consider only the disequalizing aspect, and conclude that it is probably of minor significance.

It is clear that there is much more work, both empirical and theoretical, to be done on explaining the dispersion in wage rates.

20. Hildebrand [1952-1953, p. 385]. See also Rees [1962, pp. 96-99] for a casual guess that the effect of unions is slightly disequalizing.

Fifty-five years ago, Joseph Schumpeter wrote: "The great idea of investigating the relationship between wage differences and differences in ability opens a vast perspective. The new trail is steep and stony, but it must be followed".[21] So far, it must be admitted, economists have not traveled very far along this path. The simulation results reported here suggest that the payoff to such research, in terms of increasing our understanding of the income distribution, may be quite high indeed.

21. Quoted by Staehle [1943, p. 77].

6
Some Redistributional Policies

It is therefore one of the important functions of government to prevent extreme inequality of fortunes; not by taking away wealth from its possessors, but by depriving all men of the means to accumulate it.

J.J. Rousseau

After scrutinizing the causes of inequality, it seems a natural next step to examine some policies that might alleviate this inequality. There is, of course, a great variety of possible redistributional policies: inheritance taxes and laws, various forms of progressive income taxation, negative income taxes and other income maintenance programs, wage subsidies, minimum wage legislation, educational programs of various kinds, and so on. Limitations of time, space, and the richness of the model dictate that I concentrate on only a few such policies.

The results of Chapter 5 suggest that there is relatively little payoff *in the short run* to programs that attempt to redistribute income by equalizing inherited wealth or, as an extreme case, abolishing it entirely. It was found there that a complete equalization of inheritance would lower the Gini ratio of lifetime incomes by only 0.01 -0.02. How much less, then, would any feasible reform, such as steeply progressive estate taxation, accomplish? These results imply that tracing the equalizing effects *across generations* of various estate tax schemes is not the most fruitful direction for research.[1]

On the other hand, the results obtained so far show that the payoffs to equalizing the distribution of wage rates might be quite high. This in turn suggests that some sort of wage subsidy program

1. Some such policies have been explored by Pryor [1969], using a very different simulation model.

may well be the most effective redistributive weapon now at our disposal. A variety of wage subsidy plans are simulated in Section 6.2.

At the same time, the traditional redistributional tool in the United States has been the progressive income tax; and the most popular weapon now being discussed is negative income taxation—another form of progressive income tax. For these reasons, I begin by considering the redistributional impacts of an extremely simple negative income tax.

6.1 Redistribution through Negative Income Taxes

The question at hand is, In a free-market economy where each household maximizes utility subject to a parametric wage and given tax function, how much redistribution of lifetime income can be accomplished through a negative income tax?

To answer this query, a particular type of negative income tax (NIT) must be selected from the many that have been proposed. I shall deal with a "Friedman style" negative tax, fully integrated with the personal income tax. That is, taxation is at a flat rate on all income in excess of a specified exemption; when actual income falls below the exemption level, the income tax payments are thus negative. Symbolically, the tax function is

$$T(t) = u[Y(t) - X],$$

where $T(t)$ is the tax payment, $Y(t)$ is income, u is the tax rate, and X is the exemption. Such a proposal was first propounded by Milton Friedman in his celebrated *Capitalism and Freedom* [1962, esp. pp. 174–175], and has received considerable attention since then.[2] From the standpoint of the present study, such a tax function has two important advantages. First, its simple analytical form allows it to be easily incorporated into the existing model. For each income tax rate u, a lump-sum grant equal to $\int_0^T uXe^{-rt}dt$ is added to each consumer's inheritance. Second, and perhaps more important, the present progressive tax structure in the United States can be approximated very well by such a tax function (with the exception that the minimum tax payment is zero). Thus, simulation of this negative income

2. It should be noted that most current NIT proposals do not follow Friedman's formulation. Instead, they generally include both a normal personal income tax and a separate negative income tax with a higher marginal rate.

tax scheme serves two purposes. For low levels of u and X, it gives an indication of the degree of redistribution achieved by the Federal income tax as it now stands; for higher levels of u and X, it simulates the redistributional effect of a true negative income tax.

In the terminology introduced by Musgrave [1959], I have simulated the *balanced budget incidence* of a negative income tax by the following iterative procedure. First, a tax rate was chosen, and the simulation was run with this tax rate and no lump-sum grant. This generated a budgetary surplus. Based on this surplus, a lump-sum grant—equal for each household—was made, and the simulation was repeated. If the surplus continued, the grant was raised until the budget came into balance.[3] The reader should note that this concept of budgetary balance is not the conventional annually, or even cyclically, balanced budget. It means, instead, that the taxes and expenditures made *on behalf of a particular age cohort* balance out *over the life of that cohort*. This seems to be the concept of budgetary balance appropriate to a life-cycle model. Note that with a uniform age distribution this also implies a balanced budget under the conventional definition; but for any different age distribution it does not.

In the preceding chapter I concluded that Regimes I, IIa (which allows correlation between w_0 and K_0) and IVa (which also allows correlated tastes) were probably the most realistic. These three regimes were used in all policy runs. In order to have a wide range of possible tax plans, rates ranging from 0.25 to 0.40 were considered. The lowest would be a very close approximation to the current Federal tax on individual income; the highest would be a quite radical redistributional proposal. Table 6.1 summarizes the parameters of the tax plans under consideration. Column 1 is the tax rate; column 2 is the annual exemption (X); and column 3 is the equivalent lifetime lump-sum grant per household. The next three columns summarize the distributional impacts of the tax. These results underscore the difference between the apparent and real amount of redistribution accomplished by the tax. In each case, the *real* effect is the difference between the computed Gini ratio of $K_0 + M$ and 0.295, its value in the standard case; but the *apparent* equalizing effect is the

3. The criterion for balance that I used was as follows. I assumed that the revenue generated by the 21.8% tax in the standard case was equal to the level of required government nontransfer expenditures. The budget was considered balanced under the negative income tax when the revenues from the higher tax rate, *minus all transfer payments*, left a budgetary surplus of less than one-third of 1% of nontransfer expenditures. In practice, convergence was quite rapid, and the resulting surplus was usually a fraction of the tolerated amount.

TABLE 6.1 DISTRIBUTIONAL EFFECTS OF NEGATIVE INCOME TAXES IN THE EGALITARIAN
SOCIETY (REGIME I)

	Negative Tax Plan		Gini Ratio of—			
		Equivalent		$K_0 + M$		
Tax		Lump-Sum		Minus		Before-Tax
Rate	Exemption	Grant	$K_0 + M$	Grant	M	Average M
(1)	(2)	(3)	(4)	(5)	(6)	(7)
0.218	$ 0	$ 0	0.295	0.295	0.300	$149,152
0.25	1,059	5,379	0.291	0.304	0.310	150,317
0.28	1,776	10,429	0.287	0.313	0.319	151,389
0.31	2,300	15,435	0.283	0.323	0.329	152,482
0.34	2,690	20,449	0.279	0.333	0.339	153,582
0.37	2,987	25,542	0.275	0.343	0.349	154,638
0.40	3,225	30,830	0.270	0.354	0.360	155,579

difference between the Gini ratios for after-tax lifetime incomes
$(K_0 + M)$ and incomes before government transfers $(K_0 + M -$ grant).
Finally, the last column is included to give the reader some notion of
the effect of each tax plan on the gross national product of the
simulated economy.

The overall impression given by Table 6.1 is that negative income
taxation, unless quite extreme, is not a very effective redistributor of
lifetime income. Each 3% rise in the tax rate, accompanied by the
budget-balancing exemption,[4] buys a decrease of roughly 0.004 in the
Gini ratio of lifetime incomes. The reason for such a small effect is
well known: the natural responses to redistributive taxation by
maximizing individuals are such as to disequalize the pretax distribution of income. This is illustrated by the sharp increases (about 0.01
for each 3% rise in the tax rate) in the Gini concentration ratio for
lifetime incomes, exclusive of government transfers;[5] and the similar
pattern displayed by the distribution of earnings.

The disparity between the real and apparent equalizing effects of a
negative income tax are quite clear from Table 6.1. For the least
generous tax plan, the actual drop in the Gini ratio is merely 0.004,

4. The increment in the exemption which can be financed by each tax hike of 3%
declines (from $717 between 0.25 and 0.28 to only $238 between 0.37 and 0.40) due to
the gradually increasing disincentive effects of higher tax rates.
5. This figure *does* include the proportional tax payments, but the previous chapter
showed that such a tax has a negligible effect on inequality.

but a comparison of income before government transfers and income after transfers, would indicate an apparent equalization of 0.013. For the more generous proposals the difference is even more dramatic. The 40% tax rate and accompanying grant actually reduces inequality of $K_0 + M$ by 0.025, but a comparison of incomes before and after the grant would indicate an equalization of 0.084.

With these results in mind, it is interesting to look at some statistical estimates of the effect of taxation on the size distribution of annual income. Irving Kravis [1962] has collected several pairs of pre- and post-tax distributions from the same sources for 1950. Some of his results are given in Table 6.2. The statistical effect of the tax system, it would appear, is to lower the Gini ratio of annual incomes by 0.02–0.03. The reader may accept these figures at face value if he so desires; but the simulation results suggest that the real effect of taxation is to lower the Gini ratio by only about 30% as much, that is, by less than 0.01.

Table 6.3 repeats the results of Table 6.1 for Regime IIa, the system in which wage rates have a positive correlation of 0.26 with inheritances. The figures are quite similar to those for Regime I, providing further verification of the ideas suggested there. The reduction in the Gini ratio of $K_0 + M$ ranges from an inconsequential 0.004 for the least ambitious program to 0.025 for the most radical proposal. Again, the "statistical" equalization between lifetime incomes before and after government transfers is more than twice as large.

My feeling is that a weighted average of Regimes I and IIa gives the closest approximation to the American economy. But, in deference to the strong appeal of the notion of correlated tastes, Table 6.4 offers the analogous results under Regime IVa, where labor-

TABLE 6.2 "OBSERVED" EFFECT OF TAXATION ON DISTRIBUTION: 1950

Population and Data Source	Gini Ratio of Income	
	BeforeTax	After Tax
All consumer units (Dept. of Commerce)	0.41	0.38
Urban consumer units (Bureau of Labor Statistics)	0.33	0.31
All spending units (Survey of Consumer Finances)	0.39	0.37

Source: Kravis [1962], Table 6.1, pp. 184–186.

TABLE 6.3 DISTRIBUTIONAL EFFECTS OF NEGATIVE INCOME TAXES UNDER INEQUALITY OF OPPORTUNITY (REGIME IIa)

Tax Rate	Negative Tax Plan		Gini Ratio of—			Before-Tax Average M
	Exemption	Equivalent Lump-Sum Grant	$K_0 + M$	$K_0 + M$ Minus Grant	M	
0.218	$ 0	$ 0	0.300	0.300	0.288	$148,683
0.25	1,048	5,326	0.296	0.309	0.298	149,936
0.28	1,757	10,317	0.292	0.319	0.307	150,899
0.31	2,273	15,249	0.288	0.328	0.317	151,993
0.34	2,653	20,175	0.284	0.338	0.327	153,099
0.37	2,943	25,166	0.280	0.349	0.337	154,160
0.40	3,176	30,360	0.275	0.360	0.348	155,108

TABLE 6.4 DISTRIBUTIONAL EFFECTS OF NEGATIVE INCOME TAXES IN THE STRATIFIED SOCIETY (REGIME IVa)

Tax Rate	Negative Tax Plan		Gini Ratio of—			Before-Tax Average M
	Exemption	Equivalent Lump-Sum Grant	$K_0 + M$	$K_0 + M$ Minus Grant	M	
0.218	$ 0	$ 0	0.343	0.343	0.324	$156,078
0.25	1,123	5,709	0.338	0.354	0.336	157,186
0.28	1,887	11,079	0.334	0.365	0.347	158,176
0.31	2,446	16,413	0.330	0.377	0.358	159,168
0.34	2,863	21,763	0.325	0.389	0.371	160,135
0.37	3,183	27,215	0.320	0.401	0.383	161,033
0.40	3,441	32,901	0.314	0.414	0.396	161,802

leisure tastes (ξ) are given moderate negative correlations with both w_0 and K_0. Although each tax rate can finance a larger lump-sum transfer in a regime where the high wage earners are also leisure-haters, the distributional impact of each tax plan is only slightly stronger than in the other regimes. For example, the weakest proposal lowers the Gini ratio of $K_0 + M$ by 0.005 and the strongest program lowers it by 0.029. In general, Table 6.4 corroborates the impressions gained from Tables 6.1 and 6.3.

As a final indicator of the redistributional impact of negative income taxation, more detailed than the summary Gini measure, Table 6.5 tabulates the distribution of lifetime incomes by percentiles under a moderate negative tax ($u = 0.31$) for each of the three regimes. The reader is urged to compare these results with Tables 4.4 and 4.8 which provide the same tabulations for the standard case, that is, a 21.8% proportional tax. The general impression given by this comparison is that, although the negative tax would redistribute income to only a small degree, the effect would clearly be in the right direction. In general, the lower 40%–50% of the distribution would gain at the expense of the upper 30%–40%. Not surprisingly, the very rich would not be hurt much. In fact, the upper 10% of the popula-

TABLE 6.5 LIFETIME INCOME DISTRIBUTIONS UNDER 31% NEGATIVE INCOME TAX

Population Group		Regime I Share	Regime IIa Share	Regime IVa Share
Lowest	10%	3.09%	3.06%	2.68%
Second	10%	4.89	4.83	4.30
Third	10%	6.22	6.17	5.57
Fourth	10%	7.41	7.30	6.78
Fifth	10%	8.60	8.51	7.98
Sixth	10%	9.77	9.69	9.25
Seventh	10%	11.13	11.08	10.77
Eighth	10%	12.61	12.65	12.60
Ninth	10%	15.15	15.20	15.61
Highest	10%	21.14	21.52	24.46
Top	5%	12.43	12.64	14.98
Top	1%	3.66	3.72	4.81

tion show a noticeable loss only under Regime IVa. The reason, of course, is that the steeper taxation does not touch their inherited fortunes.

6.2 Redistribution through Wage Subsidies

Recently, Jonathan Kesselman [1969] and others have proposed subsidization of low wage rates by the state as an antipoverty measure. While the motivation behind this proposal appears to have been the wage subsidy's preferred effects on work effort (that is, it is likely to be a work incentive, whereas direct grants are a disincentive), the present simulation model suggests that such subsidies may also be the only feasible way to achieve a sizable redistribution of income within a free-market system.

In this section, I consider the effects of a number of linear wage subsidy schemes. Such a plan is specified by selecting values for two parameters: the break-even wage level (w_b) and the rate of subsidization (s). Individuals with wages below w_b have their wages raised by a fraction s of the shortfall:

$$w^* = w + s(w_b - w) \quad \text{if} \quad w < w_b,$$
$$w^* = w \quad \text{if} \quad w \geqslant w_b,$$

where w is the market wage paid by the employer and w^* is the net wage received by the worker.

Manipulation of the break-even wage determines the fraction of the work force eligible for the subsidy. This, in turn, has obvious ramifications for both the overall cost of the program and the effects on labor supply. In the simulations reported below, four values were tried for w_b: $1.30, $1.60, $1.90, and $2.20. The first represents a rather austere plan whereby only the "working poor", strictly defined, are given assistance. The second contemplates partial subsidization of any worker earning less than the federal minimum wage. The two higher break-even levels lead to considerably more generous, and more costly, redistributive plans.

The subsidization rate influences both the incentive effects of the program and its cost, though it has no bearing on the number of eligible workers. Here three parameter values were experimented with: 20%, 50% and 80%. The lowest rate would represent a token subsidy plan, which should be expected to have only minimal effects on equality and output. The 50% rate is, perhaps, the most relevant policy alternative, while the 80% rate is tried to give some idea of the potential equalizing effect of near-complete wage subsidization.

It should be emphasized at the outset that the results to follow underestimate the costs and overestimate the distributional impacts of such a subsidy program by considering only the supply side and ignoring the demand for labor. It is clear that employers in markets now in equilibrium with wage rates below the breakeven level would lower their wage offers if they knew that employees would treat any wage offer below w_b as if it were $w + s(w_b - w)$, that is, if the supply curve of labor were steeper below w_b per hour. Figure 6.1a illustrates that, as long as demand for labor is not infinitely elastic at the prevailing wage, institution of the proposed wage subsidy would result in a lowering of market wages in those markets now paying less than w_b. Figure 6.1b illustrates that there would be no effect on those markets now reaching equilibrium at wages above w_b. In Figure 6.1a the amount by which w_1 (market wage after subsidy) falls short of w_0 (market wage before subsidy) depends on the elasticities of supply and demand. In general, it is a more serious problem the greater the elasticity of supply and the lower the elasticity of demand. Of course, for wage subsidy plans which employ lower subsidization rates, this is less of a problem.

In all simulations, the break-even wage level is assumed to be a relative concept, that is, the w_b is assumed to rise at the trend rate of increase of real wages, 1.64% per annum. Thus, in the model, a person never leaves the wage subsidy rolls. On this score, the simulation may be thought to give an overestimate of costs. In discussions of wage subsidies and other income maintenance programs, the hope is often expressed that subsidization will lead to "rising expectations" and thus to efforts to raise one's productivity, thereby lowering one's subsidy. The model does not allow for such psychological effects.

The iterative procedure followed to balance the budget is similar to the one for negative taxes. First, a break-even level and a subsidization rate are selected and the costs of the program under the 21.8% tax rate are computed. This result is used to estimate the tax increase needed to finance the subsidy plan[6] and the simulation is run again with the higher tax rate. If the budget is still in the red, the tax rate is raised again. The process is halted when the budgetary deficit is less than one-third of 1% of the original (no-subsidy) budget.

The results obtained for Regime I are summarized in Table 6.6. Some explanation of the variables listed there may be in order.

6. Note that part of the subsidy is recouped through income taxation.

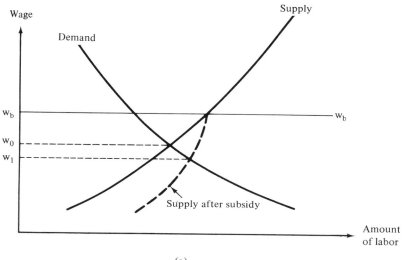

(a)

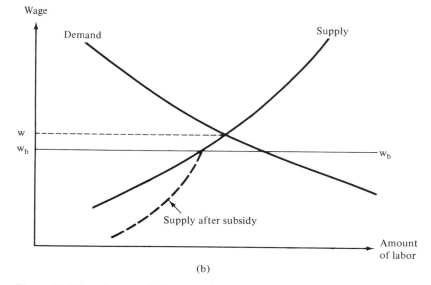

(b)

Figure 6.1 Effect of wage subsidy on market wages

TABLE 6.6 DISTRIBUTIONAL EFFECTS OF WAGE SUBSIDY PLANS IN THE EGALITARIAN SOCIETY

Break-Even Wage (1)	Subsidy Rate (2)	Fraction of Population Subsidized (3)	Income Tax Rate to Balance Budget (4)	Cost Per Family (5)	Equivalent Annual Cost (6)	Gini Ratio of— $K_0 + M$ (7)	M (8)	Before-Tax Average M (9)
None	—	0	0.218	0	0	0.295	0.295	$149,152
$1.30	20%	14.8%	0.220	$ 471	$ 29	0.290	0.296	$150,142
	50%		0.223	1,185	74	0.283	0.288	151,561
	80%		0.227	1,906	119	0.277	0.282	153,226
$1.60	20%	21.5%	0.222	$ 949	$ 59	0.286	0.292	$151,136
	50%		0.229	2,389	149	0.273	0.278	154,213
	80%		0.235	3,840	239	0.261	0.266	157,226
$1.90	20%	30.8%	0.225	$ 1,644	$103	0.280	0.286	$152,581
	50%		0.236	4,138	258	0.260	0.265	157,818
	80%		0.246	6,649	414	0.242	0.246	163,045
$2.20	20%	39.5%	0.229	$ 2,570	$160	0.274	0.279	$154,499
	50%		0.245	6,464	403	0.246	0.250	162,621
	80%		0.260	10,378	647	0.222	0.226	170,897

Columns 4–6 give three different indications of the costs of the wage subsidy program. Column 5 ("Cost per family") is obtained simply by dividing the out-of-pocket costs of the wage subsidies (*not* considering the extra tax revenues returned) by the number of households in the sample. Column 6 converts this lifetime total to an equivalent *annual cost* (per household) to the government.[7] For example, for the plan with a $1.30 break-even level and a 20% subsidy rate, the total life-cycle cost of the wage subsidy program is equivalent to $29 per household per year over the 54.7 year life of the age cohort. The last column is again included to give some crude notion of the effect of the policy on the GNP.

Though admittedly biased in their favor, the results in columns 7 and 8 of Table 6.6 give proponents of the wage subsidy at least modest grounds for optimism. For example, with the same 25% income tax rate that bought only a trivial equalization under the NIT

---

7. In making this calculation, the government was assumed to discount future tax receipts at the pre-tax rate of return, 6%.

(see Table 6.1), it would be possible to subsidize wages below $1.90 at better than an 80% rate, or wages below $2.20 at more than 50%. Either of these programs would drive the Gini ratio for lifetime incomes down to about 0.24—a reduction in inequality of about 19%. Even assuming, as a rough approximation, that ignoring demand elasticities biases these estimates toward optimism by a factor of three, the indication is that either of these wage subsidies would reduce the Gini ratio about 0.018, as compared to the 0.004 reduction from the NIT of the same cost.

The subsidy schemes which seem most within the realm of political feasibility are perhaps 80% subsidization of wages below $1.30 or 50% subsidies to wages less than $1.60. The former, which could be financed by a one percentage point hike in the personal income tax rate, would reduce inequality some 0.018 at a gross budgetary cost equivalent to $119 per family per year. To accomplish this much equalization under the NIT would require a tax rate of about 35.5% according to Table 6.1. If I again scale down the indicated drop in inequality from the wage subsidy by two-thirds, the indicated NIT tax rate is about 26.5%. Subsidizing 50% of the shortfall of wages from the federal minimum wage would, according to Table 6.6, lower the Gini ratio of income to 0.273, which is lower than that obtained with a 37% negative income tax. And it could be financed by a 23% income tax rate. Applying the same discount factor as before, I might realistically equate this subsidy with a 27% NIT.

The reasons for the superior redistributional potential of wage suubsidies over negative income taxes are clear enough. In the first place, all the aid goes to the lower part of the income distribution, that is, to persons with wage rates below the break-even level.[8] A negative income tax, on the other hand, is equivalent to an equal lump-sum grant to every family, regardless of need. Secondly, since higher wages are a work incentive to those on the subsidy, wage subsidization actually equalizes the distribution of market earnings (see column 8 of Table 6.6). By contrast, negative income taxes always make earnings more disperse (see column 6 of Table 6.1).[9]

Table 6.7 shows that the distributional impacts of the various wage subsidy programs are virtually identical under Regime IIa, while the budgetary costs are (very) slightly higher.

8. This statement is valid only when, as in the present model, there are no multi-earner families.
9. No attention is paid here to the grave administrative problems in implementing a wage subsidy plan. Suffice it to say that most people view them as more serious than those that beset the NIT.

TABLE 6.7 DISTRIBUTIONAL EFFECTS OF WAGE SUBSIDY PLANS UNDER INEQUALITY OF OPPORTUNITY (REGIME IIa)

Break-Even Wage (1)	Subsidy Rate (2)	Fraction of Population Subsidized (3)	Income Tax Rate to Balance Budget (4)	Cost Per Family (5)	Equivalent Annual Cost (6)	Gini Ratio of— $K_0 + M$ (7)	M (8)	Before-Tax Average M (9)
None	—	0	0.218	0	0	0.300	0.288	$148,683
$1.30	20%	14.8%	0.220	$ 485	$ 30	0.295	0.284	$149,640
	50%		0.224	1,215	76	0.288	0.276	151,281
	80%		0.227	1,947	121	0.282	0.270	152,746
$1.60	20%	21.5%	0.222	$ 975	$ 61	0.291	0.279	$150,612
	50%		0.230	2,444	152	0.278	0.266	153,928
	80%		0.235	3,917	244	0.266	0.254	156,734
$1.90	20%	30.8%	0.226	$ 1,690	$105	0.286	0.273	$152,251
	50%		0.237	4,233	264	0.265	0.253	157,540
	80%		0.247	6,780	423	0.247	0.234	162,765
$2.20	20%	39.5%	0.230	$ 2,636	$164	0.279	0.269	$154,190
	50%		0.246	6,598	411	0.250	0.238	162,348
	80%		0.262	10,562	658	0.226	0.214	170,856

Finally, Table 6.8 presents these same data for Regime IVa, the inegalitarian case where both wages and tastes are correlated. The differences are not very great. In general, each wage subsidy program is a slightly less effective redistributor because the low wage individuals are leisure lovers.[10] By the same token, however, each subsidy level can be financed by a lower tax rate because the rich are inherently harder workers. So wage subsidization appears to be about as effective a redistributional measure as in the other regimes.

Table 6.9 goes beyond the Gini ratio to consider the full income distribution under each regime. Since the $1.60 break-even level with a 50% subsidization rate seems the most interesting, each distribution in Table 6.9 is calculated on the basis of this plan. The resulting distributions may usefully be compared with the standard case.[11] It is apparent that the poorest deciles are the biggest potential gainers

10. One may perhaps reasonably expect some reinforcing changes in tastes here as the "cycle of poverty" is broken.
11. See Tables 4.4 and 4.8.

TABLE 6.8 DISTRIBUTIONAL EFFECTS OF WAGE SUBSIDY PLANS IN THE STRATIFIED SOCIETY (REGIME IVa)

Break-Even Wage (1)	Subsidy Rate (2)	Fraction of Population Subsidized (3)	Income Tax Rate to Balance Budget (4)	Cost Per Family (5)	Equivalent Annual Cost (6)	Gini Ratio of—		Before-Tax Average
						$K_0 + M$ (7)	M (8)	M (9)
None	—	0	0.218	0	0	0.343	0.324	$156,078
$1.30	20%	14.8%	0.220	$ 424	$ 26	0.338	0.320	$156,983
	50%		0.223	1,064	66	0.332	0.314	158,350
	80%		0.225	1,706	106	0.326	0.308	159,529
$1.60	20%	21.5%	0.222	$ 862	$ 54	0.335	0.316	$157,910
	50%		0.228	2,159	135	0.323	0.304	160,680
	80%		0.233	3,461	216	0.312	0.293	163,320
$1.90	20%	30.8%	0.224	$1,507	$ 94	0.329	0.311	$159,094
	50%		0.234	3,776	235	0.310	0.291	163,927
	80%		0.242	6,051	377	0.293	0.273	168,463
$2.20	20%	39.5%	0.228	$2,371	$148	0.323	0.304	$160,967
	50%		0.242	5,937	370	0.296	0.277	168,322
	80%		0.256	9,507	593	0.272	0.252	175,951

from such a reform. Compared to the standard case, in Regime I the bottom 20% of the distribution increases its share by over 1.5 percentage points, while the upper seven deciles are net losers. However, a closer look at the upper tail reveals, once again, that the very rich have not lost ground. The top 5% have suffered a rather meager reduction in their share, while the top 1% has scarcely lost at all. The explanation, I suppose, is that these extremely rich individuals have large inheritances, which are not touched by taxation. This redistributional pattern is more or less replicated in Regimes IIa and IVa. In a word, the redistribution accomplished by the wage subsidy system is certainly in the right direction, with the possible exception that the very rich do not pay their fair share.

6.3 Concluding Remark

It would appear, then, from the simulation results that wage subsidies are—at least potentially—more powerful redistributors than negative

TABLE 6.9 LIFETIME INCOME DISTRIBUTION UNDER 50% SUBSIDY
FOR WAGES BELOW $1.60

Population Group		Regime I Share	Regime IIa Share	Regime IVa Share
Lowest	10%	3.94%	3.92%	3.43%
Second	10%	5.06	5.01	4.42
Third	10%	6.15	6.10	5.48
Fourth	10%	7.24	7.12	6.56
Fifth	10%	8.41	8.30	7.77
Sixth	10%	9.58	9.50	9.08
Seventh	10%	10.97	10.91	10.63
Eighth	10%	12.48	12.50	12.50
Ninth	10%	15.08	15.12	15.55
Highest	10%	21.10	21.51	24.57
Top	5%	12.40	12.66	15.09
Top	1%	3.62	3.70	4.88

income taxes.[12] And this result has been obtained even though the elasticity of supply of labor is relatively low in this model; a model with higher supply elasticities would, of course, show even more lopsided results in favor of subsidizing wages. However, a quantitative assessment of the superiority of the wage subsidy is not really possible within the confines of the present model, as there is no way of determining how far the market wages paid by employers would fall were a wage subsidy inaugurated. As a crude adjustment for this, I have scaled down the indicated redistribution achieved by each subsidy by two-thirds in making comparisons between wage subsidies and negative income taxes. Whether this is an over- or under-adjustment remains an open question that can only be answered by a full general-equilibrium model.

12. Similar conclusions have been reached by Kesselman [1973], using a simulation model derived from the optimal-income-tax framework of Mirrlees [1971].

7
Conclusions

That democracy and extreme economic inequality form, when combined, an unstable compound, is no novel doctrine.

R.H. Tawney

7.1 Review of Findings

In these pages a microeconomic simulation model of the size distribution of income and wealth in the United States is developed, tested, and used to answer several important questions pertaining to the causes, and possible alleviation, of inequality.

Starting from the accounting identity that for each person at every point in time,

$$Y = wh + rK,$$

where Y is income, w is the wage rate, h denotes hours of work, r is the interest rate, and K is net worth, I argue (Chapter 1) that a rigorous economic theory of income distribution should be built up from precise models of individual choices of w, h, r, and k. Such models, based on utility-maximizing behavior, would yield solutions for each person's wage rate, labor supply, rate of return, and net worth, contingent upon his tastes and endowments of human and nonhuman capital. Given such models, it would be possible to compute the income or wealth distribution from any assumed distributions of tastes and endowments. Doubtless the resulting income distribution would be too complex to write down in any closed analytical form. Hence the resort to numerical simulation.

The model presented here meets only a portion of these rather demanding requirements; the life-cycle patterns of labor supply and capital accumulation are derived from a model of intertemporal utility maximization, but wages and rates of return are assumed to be exogenous (Chapters 2 and 3). Some sort of human-capital model to generate the life-cycle pattern of w, and a dynamic portfolio-selection model to determine the r for each individual are needed to complete the picture. While neither is attempted here, I suggest in Chapter 2 that the latter might not be too hard to achieve. The former, however, presents a formidable problem.

Recognizing the limitations of the model, it is worthwhile reviewing some of the questions with which it has been confronted and the answers it has given.

The initial, and most basic, query is whether such an abstract model of a perfectly functioning competitive economy can possibly produce the degree of inequality observed in modern mixed economies. After all, it has no involuntary unemployment, no capital gains or losses, no entrepreneurial income, and so on. The tentative answer is that it can, at least as long as the distribution of tastes is given considerable dispersion (Chapter 4). In fact, with the assumed dispersion in tastes, regimes where the relative preference for leisure is negatively correlated with endowments actually generate more inequality than is found in U.S. data. This, of course, does not mean that tastes are uncorrelated, but simply that the model with correlated tastes can replicate the American income distribution only with a more concentrated distribution of tastes than is employed. Interestingly, the simulation results show that overall income inequality is not affected much by "inequality of opportunity" as defined here, that is, by positive correlation between wages and inherited wealth.

Perhaps more important from a social point of view than the *amount* of inequality (however measured) are the *causes* of this inequality. An extremely unequal distribution caused strictly by differences in tastes poses no social problems, whereas a smaller degree of inequality attributable entirely to inherited wealth does. I therefore use the model to decompose the total simulated inequality (as measured by the Gini ratio) into the portions contributed by differences in tastes, unequal wage rates, and the unequal distribution of inherited wealth (Chapter 5). Two striking conclusions emerge in every regime. First, inheritances account for surprisingly little overall inequality. Presumably this is because of their small average size as compared with earned income, and because the receipt of a large inheritance can be a powerful work disincentive. Second, dispersion in wage rates is always the principal cause of inequality—a finding with important consequences for both policy and research. From the policy standpoint, it suggests that the most effective way to equalize incomes is to pursue programs that attempt to equalize wages. Compensatory education, wage subsidies, and antidiscrimination legislation are a few obvious candidates. To the researcher, it suggests that more resources should be devoted to achieving a better theoretical and empirical understanding of the causes of inequality in wage rates.

A crude start along this path is made by some experiments that attempt to simulate the distributional effects of an end to race or sex discrimination in wages, or to union-nonunion wage differentials. The potential equalization achievable by equalizing the average wages of blacks and whites (while keeping the shapes of the distributions unchanged) turns out to be surprisingly small—a reduction in the Gini ratio of about 0.01. The results for obliterating male-female wage differentials are even more striking: essentially no equalization is accomplished. Ending union-nonunion differentials leads to about as much equalization as ending race differentials. However, as noted in Section 5.2, these disappointing results give no reason to be pessimistic about redistributional policies that concentrate their benefits on *low-wage* blacks, or *low-wage* women, or *low-wage* nonunion workers rather than giving equiproportionate benefits to all members of the "disadvantaged" group.

It has often been noted that, because of typical life-cycle patterns in income, distributions of annual income display more inequality than would be found in the distribution of income over some longer period such as the lifetime.[1] However, the quantitative importance of this phenomenon is not known. How much of the observed inequality in the size distribution of annual income in the United States is simply attributable to the fact that the population consists of people of different ages? The model can shed some light on this important question by using the actual age distribution of the U.S. population to compute a distribution of annual incomes. Comparing this with the lifetime income distributions for a single age cohort suggests that about 30% of the observed inequality is attributable to life-cycle influences. The simulated annual income distributions are also compared with actual U.S. data, and the concordance is found to be remarkable.

1. Another reason for this is that annual incomes contain transitory components that wash out over longer accounting periods. But this phenomenon does not appear in the model.

Finally, some frequently discussed tax-and-transfer schemes to redistribute income are incorporated into the model (Chapter 6). It is found that linear negative income taxes hold little hope for achieving a substantial redistribution. The reason is simply that the distribution of income before negative tax payments gets successively more unequal as the generosity of the negative tax plan increases. Here looks can be very deceiving. Comparison of the post- and pre-transfer distributions often suggests a large reduction in inequality, though the difference between the post-transfer distribution and the distribution in the absence of transfers is quite small. The simulation results are much more sanguine on the possibility of redistribution through wage subsidies, indicating that quite substantial reductions in inequality are obtainable at reasonable budgetary cost. However, these calculations are too optimistic, since they ignore the demand side of the low-wage labor markets. The knowledge that low wages are to be subsidized by the government would surely induce employers to reduce these wages, thus aggravating the inequality in pre-subsidy wage rates. The extent of this cannnot be examined within the confines of the present model. But even assuming that the model overstates the redistributional potential of wage subsidies by a factor of three (which seems like a large adjustment) does not overturn the conclusion that wage subsidies are a much more effective redistributional device than negative income taxes.

7.2 Directions for Future Research

Since many shortcomings of the model in its present form have become obvious in the course of this study, a large number of potential directions for future research have been pinpointed. And I believe the results obtained with even so simple a model have been sufficiently encouraging to suggest that the payoff to pursuing at least some of these extensions may be considerable.

One obvious empirical question raised by the substantial distributional differences among the different regimes is, Which regime most closely approximates the United States? The simulations reported here suggest that the most important unknown parameter is the correlation of the taste for leisure with wage rates and/or inheritances. Since this is not directly observable, extracting this information from empirical data is a challenging problem—and a potentially important one. Once the degree to which tastes are "programmed" has been measured, attention can be turned to the channels through which these tastes are determined.

One of the important findings of the model—that unequal inheritances account for relatively little income inequality—rests on a rather weak data base. As this has rather important policy implications, it would be desirable to obtain better data on the distribution of inherited wealth. Since the shape of this important distribution is almost unknown at present, these data would be useful for other purposes as well.

The promising results obtained in simulating the redistributional effects of wage subsidies, as compared wth negative income taxes, suggests still another area of empirical research: the labor-supply responses of individuals to wage subsidization. Over the past several years escalating interest in the NIT as an antipoverty program has led to a number of cross-sectional studies of labor supply functions including, but not limited to, those that have been derived from the federally sponsored negative income tax experiments.[2] These results have been and will continue to be used to estimate the costs and distributional benefits of various NIT plans. It would be useful to employ these same data sources and labor supply functions to estimate the costs and benefits of wage subsidy plans of the kind considered here.

But by far the most important area for empirical research is suggested by the persistent finding that wage inequality is the chief cause of income inequality. While there has been considerable work done on the question of why wages differ,[3] the field is by no means closed.

Each of these areas where empirical knowledge is weak or nonexistent is certainly important, but the deficiencies in the theoretical basis of the model are probably even more serious.

The theoretical spadework necessary to fill some of the gaps in the model has already been done, so that the simulation apparatus can in principle be expanded to incorporate them. For example, the present model develops only the supply sides of the labor and capital markets, treating the wage level and interest rate as exogenous. A general equilibrium version of the model would also generate demand functions for capital and labor deduced from the behavior of firms. This extension is particularly important for analysis of the wage subsidy, where the present model allows me only to guess the probable reduction in the market wages brought about by inauguration of the subsidy.

2. Several of these studies have been collected in Cain and Watts [1973], but there are others both published and in preparation.
3. See the references cited in footnote 12, Chapter 1.

Another example is the treatment of property income. The volume of savings by each individual is rigorously derived from lifetime utility maximization, but the allocation of these savings among different assets with different yields is simply ignored by assuming that there is only one asset with a known yield. It is well known that the rich earn a better average return on invested capital than the poor, and the main reason is that the two groups hold portfolios of radically different composition. Of course, it makes little sense to introduce a multiplicity of assets into a certainty model; if all assets have the same yield, there might as well be only one asset. So this requires the adoption of some lifetime portfolio-selection model under uncertainty. Such models, generally based on the expected utility hypothesis, have been developed and integrated with consumption-savings decisions such as those analyzed in Chapter 2.[4] Whether such portfolio choices can easily be accommodated in a model like that of Chapter 3, which includes labor-leisure choices as well, remains an open question.

Once uncertainty has been introduced there seems to be little reason to confine it to uncertainty over rates of return. Few people know with complete certainty the wage rates they will be able to earn in the future. There is hardly any theory of labor-leisure choices under uncertainty[5] and, to my knowledge, none that attempts to extend it into a dynamic life-cycle context. Fewer people still know for sure the length of their lives. Here the necessary theoretical work has already been done for models that ignore labor-leisure choices[6] but not for models as complex as that of Chapter 3. In a word, there is a great deal of basic theoretical work necessary before a full-blown uncertainty version of the present simulation model can be developed.

Returning to the realm of certainty, the most significant gap in the present theoretical structure of the model is undoubtedly the assumption that wages are exogenous. That is, there is no possibility of altering one's future wage rate by investing in human capital. While there is a considerable literature on human capital theory,[7] some of it even applicable to life-cycle problems,[8] it could not be exploited for

---

4. See, for example, Hakansson [1970], Merton [1969], and Samuelson[1969].
5. Block and Heineke [1973] extend the neoclassical theory of labor-leisure choice into an uncertainty context by utilizing the expected utility hypothesis.
6. Yaari [1965], Atkinson [1971b].
7. Among the many references that could be cited see Becker [1962, 1964, 1967], and Mincer [1958, 1970].
8. Ben-Porath [1967, 1970].

use in the present model because none of this literature considers labor-leisure choices. In the present state of the art, the investigator must choose between analyzing the labor-training choice and ignoring leisure (as the human capital theorists have done), or analyzing labor-leisure choice and ignoring training (as I have done). Integration of the present model with a life-cycle version of human-capital theory would be a major breakthrough.

Finally, it is easy to think of a variety of other real-world influences on the income distribution which have not been dealt with here. For example, progressive income and estate taxation certainly accomplishes some equalization. In Chapter 2, I noted how a specific form of progressive estate tax could be incorporated into the model with no great difficulty; but it is by no means obvious how a progressive income tax could be dealt with. The uneven incidence of unemployment is another phenomena which may be important for understanding inequality in the United States, but about which relatively little is known. Finally, race discrimination, sex discrimination, and unionization are dealt with in a crudely empirical manner in Chapter 5. It would be more desirable to integrate these real-world phenomena somehow into the underlying theoretical structure of the model.

In brief, even within the framework presented in this book, there is a great deal of work to be done before a comprehensive and rigorous economic theory of income distribution can be said to exist. In addition, entirely different theoretical frameworks are possible. The theory of size distribution is indeed still in its infancy.

Bibliography

Aitchison, J. and J. A. C. Brown, 1954.
"On Criteria for Descriptions of Income Distribution," *Metroeconomica* 6: 88–107.

————, 1957.
The Lognormal Distribution. Cambridge, England: Cambridge University Press.

Ammon, Otto, 1899.
"Some Social Applications of The Doctrine of Probability," *Journal of Political Economy* 7: 204–237. (Translated from German by Carlos C. Closson).

Atkinson, A. B., 1971a.
"Capital Taxes, the Redistribution of Wealth and Individual Savings," *Review of Economic Studies* 38: 209–228.

————, 1971b.
"The Distribution of Wealth and the Individual Life-Cycle," *Oxford Economic Papers* 23: 239–254.

Becker, Gary S., 1962.
"Investment in Human Capital: A Theoretical Analysis," *Journal of Political Economy* 70 (Supplement): 9–49.

————, 1964.
Human Capital: A Theoretical and Empirical Analysis with Special Reference to Education. New York: Columbia University Press for NBER.

————, 1965.
"A Theory of the Allocation of Time," *Economic Journal* 75: 493–517.

————, 1967.
Human Capital and the Personal Distribution of Income: An Analytical Approach. W. S. Woytinsky Lecture No. 1. Ann Arbor, Mich.: University of Michigan.

Becker, Gary S. and Barry R. Chiswick, 1966.
"Education and the Distribution of Earnings," *American Economic Review, Papers and Proceedings* 56: 358–369.

Ben-Porath, Yoram, 1967.
"The Production of Human Capital and the Life-Cycle of Earnings," *Journal of Political Economy* 75: 353–365.

————, 1970.
"The Production of Human Capital over Time," in W. L. Hansen (ed.), *Education, Income and Human Capital*. New York: Columbia University Press for NBER.

Bewley, Truman F., 1972.
"Existence of Equilibria in Economies with Infinitely Many Commodities," *Journal of Economic Theory* 4: 514–540.

Bjerke, Kjeld, 1961.
"Some Income and Wage Distribution Theories: Summary and Comments," *Weltwirtschaftliches Archiv* 86: 46–66.

Blinder, Alan S., 1971.
"Estimating a Micro Wage Equation: Pitfalls and Some Provisional Estimates," *Research Memorandum No. 131*, Princeton: Econometric Research Program.

————, 1973a.
"Wage Discrimination: Reduced Form and Structural Estimates," *Journal of Human Resources* 8: 436–455.

————, 1973b.
"A Model of Inherited Wealth," *Quarterly Journal of Economics* 87: 608–626.

Block, M. K. and J. M. Heineke, 1973.
"The Allocation of Effort under Uncertainty: The Case of Risk-averse Behavior," *Journal of Political Economy* 81: 376-385.

Boissevain, C. H., 1939.
"Distribution of Abilities Depending upon Two or More Independent Factors," *Metron* 13: 49-58.

Boskin, Michael J., 1972.
"Unions and Relative Real Wages," *American Economic Review* 62: 466–472.

Bowles, Samuel, 1972.
"Schooling and Inequality from Generation to Generation," *Journal of Political Economy* 80 (Supplement): S219–S251.

Bryson, Arthur and Yu-Chi Ho, 1969.
Applied Optimal Control. Waltham, Mass: Blaisdell.

Budd, Edward C., 1970.
"Postwar Changes in the Size Distribution of Income in the U.S.," *American Economic Review, Papers and Proceedings* 60: 247–260.

Cain, Glen and Harold Watts, 1973.
Labor Supply and Income Maintenance. Chicago: Markham.

Champernowne, David G., 1953.
"A Model of Income Distribution," *Economic Journal* 63: 318–351.

Chiswick, Barry R. and Jacob Mincer, 1972.
"Time–Series Changes in Personal Income Inequality in the United States from 1939, with Projections to 1985," *Journal of Political Economy* 80 (Supplement): S34–S66.

Denison, Edward F., 1954.
"Income Types and the Size Distribution," *American Economic Review, Papers and Proceedings* 44: 254–269.

Dorfman, Robert, 1969.
"An Economic Interpretation of Optimal Control Theory," *American Economic Review* 59: 817–831.

Duncan, Otis Dudley, 1968.
"Ability and Achievement," *Eugenics Quarterly* 15: 1–11.

Fair, Ray C., 1971.
"The Optimal Distribution of Income," *Quarterly Journal of Economics* 85: 551–579.

Fiekowsky, Seymour, 1956.
"On the Significance of Successors' Welfare as a Motivation for the Accumulation of Wealth," *Proceedings of the Western Economic Association* 6: 42–48.

———, 1966.
"The Effect on Saving of the United States Estate and Gift Tax," in C.S. Shoup (ed.), *Federal Estate and Gift Taxes*. Washington D.C.: Brookings Institution.

French, Richard E., 1970.
An Estimate of Personal Wealth in Oklahoma in 1960. Gainesville, Fla.: University of Florida Press.

Friedman, Milton, 1953.
"Choice, Chance and the Personal Distribution of Income," *Journal of Political Economy* 61: 273–290.

———, 1957.
A Theory of the Consumption Function. Princeton, N.J.: Princeton University Press for NBER.

———, 1962.
Capitalism and Freedom. Chicago: University of Chicago Press.

Gallman, Robert E., 1969.
"Trends in the Size Distribution of Wealth in the Nineteenth Century: Some Speculations," in L. Soltow (ed.), *Six Papers on the Size Distribution of Wealth and Income*. New York: Columbia University Press for NBER.

Gastwirth, Joseph L., 1972.
"The Estimation of the Lorenz Curve and the Gini Index," *Review of Economics and Statistics* 54: 306–316.

Gibrat, Robert, 1957.
"On Economic Inequalities," *International Economic Papers* 7: 53–70. (Translated from the 1931 French edition.)

Gintis, Herbert, 1971.
"Education, Technology and the Characteristics of Worker Productivity," *American Economic Review, Papers and Proceedings* 61: 266–279.

Goldman, Steven M., 1969.
"Consumption Behavior and Time Preference," *Journal of Economic Theory* 1: 39–47.

Goldsmith, Selma F., 1957.
"Changes in the Size Distribution of Income," *American Economic Review, Papers and Proceedings* 47: 504–518.

Griliches, Zvi, 1970.
"Notes on the Role of Education in Production Functions and Growth Accounting," in W. L. Hansen (ed.), *Education, Income and Human Capital*. New York: Columbia University Press for NBER.

Griliches, Zvi and William M. Mason, 1972.
"Education, Income, and Ability," *Journal of Political Economy* 80 (Supplement): S74–S103.

Hakansson, Nils H., 1970.
"Optimal Investment and Consumption Strategies under Risk for a Class of Utility Functions," *Econometrica* 38: 587–607.

Haldane, J. B. S., 1942.
"Moments of the Distributions of Powers and Products of Normal Variates," *Biometrika* 32: 226–242.

Haley, Bernard F., 1968.
"Changes in the Distribution of Income in the U.S.," in J. Marchal and B. Ducros (eds.), *The Distribution of National Income*. New York: International Economic Association.

Hall, Robert E., 1973.
"Wages, Income and Hours of Work in the U.S. Labor Force," in G. Cain and H. Watts (eds.), *Labor Supply and Income Maintenance*. Chicago: Markham.

Harrington, Michael, 1962.
The Other America. New York: Macmillan.

Hause, John C., 1972.
"Earnings Profile: Ability and Schooling," *Journal of Political Economy* 80 (Supplement), S108–S138.

Hicks, John R., 1946.
Value and Capital, Second Edition. Oxford: The Clarendon Press.

Hildebrand, George H., 1952–1953.
"American Unionism, Social Stratification, and Power," *American Journal of Sociology* 58: 381–390.

Hurd, Michael D., 1971.
"Changes in Wage Rates between 1959 and 1967," *Review of Economics and Statistics* 53: 189–199.

Ishikawa, Tsuneo, forthcoming.
"Imperfection in the Capital Market and the Institutional Arrangement of Inheritance," *Review of Economic Studies*, in press.

Jencks, Christopher et al., 1972.
Inequality: A Reassessment of the Effect of Family and Schooling in America. New York: Basic Books.

Kalecki, M. 1945.
"On the Gibrat Distribution," *Econometrica* 13: 161–170.

Kesselman, Jonathan, 1969.
"Labor-Supply Effects of Income, Income-Work, and Wage Subsidies," *Journal of Human Resources* 4: 275–292.

———, 1973.
"Optimal Taxation of Individual Ability," mimeo, University of British Columbia.

Kravis, Irving B., 1962.
The Structure of Income. Philadelphia: University of Pennsylvania.

Lampman, Robert J., 1962.
The Share of Top Wealth-Holders in National Wealth, 1922–56. Princeton, N.J.: Princeton University Press for NBER.

Lansing, John B. and John Sonquist, 1969.
"A Cohort Analysis of Changes in the Distribution of Wealth," in L. Soltow (ed.), *Six Papers on The Size Distribution of Wealth and Income*. New York: Columbia University Press for NBER.

Levhari, David and T. N. Srinivasan, 1969.
"Optimal Savings under Uncertainty," *Review of Economic Studies* 36: 153–163.

Lydall, Harold F., 1959.
"The Distribution of Employment Incomes," *Econometrica* 27:110–115.

———, 1968.
The Structure of Earnings. Oxford: The Clarendon Press.

Malkiel, Burton G. and Judith A. Malkiel, 1973.
"Male-Female Pay Differentials in Professional Employment," *American Economic Review* 63: 693–705.

Mandelbrot, Benoit, 1960.
"The Pareto-Lévy Law and the Distribution of Income," *International Economic Review* 1: 79–106.

———, 1961.
"Stable Paretian Random Functions and the Multiplicative Variation of Income," *Econometrica* 29: 517–543.

———, 1962.
"Paretian Distributions and Income Maximization," *Quarterly Journal of Economics* 76: 57–85.

Mayer, Thomas, 1960.
"The Distribution of Ability and Earnings," *Review of Economics and Statistics* 42: 189–195.

Merton, Robert C., 1969.
"Lifetime Portfolio Selection Under Uncertainty: The Continuous-Time Case," *Review of Economics and Statistics* 51: 247–257.

Miller, Herman P., 1955a.
Income of the American People. New York: John Wiley.

———, 1955b.
"Elements of Symmetry in the Skewed Income Curve," *Journal of the American Statistical Association* 50: 55–71.

Mincer, Jacob, 1958.
"Investment in Human Capital and Personal Income Distribution," *Journal of Political Economy* 66: 281–302.

———, 1970.
"The Distribution of Labor Incomes: A Survey with Special Reference to the Human Capital Approach," *Journal of Economic Literature* 8: 1–26.

Mirrlees, James A., 1971.
"An Exploration in the Theory of Optimum Income Taxation," *Review of Economic Studies* 38: 175–208.

Modigliani, Franco and Richard Brumberg, 1954.
"Utility Analysis and the Consumption Function: An Interpretation of Cross-Section Data," in K. K. Kurihara (ed.), *Post-Keynesian Economics.* New Brunswick, N.J.: Rutgers University Press.

Morgan, James N., Martin H. David, Wilber J. Cohen, and Harvey Brazer, 1962.
Income and Welfare in the United States. New York: McGraw-Hill.

Morgan, James N. and James O. Smith, 1969.
A Panel Study of Income Dynamics: Study Design, Procedures, and Forms; 1969 Interviewing Year (Wave II). Ann Arbor: Survey Research Center.

Musgrave, Richard A., 1959.
The Theory of Public Finance. New York: McGraw-Hill.

Oaxaca, Ronald, 1973.
"Sex Discrimination in Wages," in O. C. Ashenfelter and A. Rees (eds.), *Discrimination in Labor Markets.* Princeton, N.J.: Princeton University Press.

Pechman, Joseph A. 1966.
Federal Tax Policy. Washington: The Brookings Institution.

Phelps, Edmund S., 1962.
"The Accumulation of Risky Capital: A Sequential Utility Analysis," *Econometrica* 30: 729–743.

Pigou, A. C., 1924.
The Economics of Welfare, Second Edition. London: Macmillan.

Pollak, Robert A., 1970.
"Homogeneous von Neumann-Morgenstern Utility Functions," *International Economic Review* 11: 117–130.

Pontryagin, L. S., V. C. Boltyanskii, R. V. Gamkrelidze and E. F. Mishchenko, 1962.
The Mathematical Theory of Optimal Processes. New York: Interscience.

Pratt, John W., 1964.
"Risk Aversion in the Small and in the Large," *Econometrica* 32: 122–136.

Projector, Dorothy S. and Gertrude S. Weiss, 1966.
Survey of Financial Characteristics of Consumers. Washington: Board of Governors of the Federal Reserve System.

Projector, Dorothy S., Gertrude S. Weiss, and Erling T. Thoresen, 1969.
"Composition of Income as Shown by the Survey of Financial Characteristics of Consumers," in L. Soltow (ed.), *Six Papers on the Size Distribution of Wealth and Income*. New York: Columbia University Press for NBER.

Pryor, Frederic L., 1969.
"The Impact of Social and Economic Institutions on the Size Distribution of Income and Wealth: A Simulation Study," paper read at the December 1969 meetings of the American Economic Association in New York. A modified version was published in *American Economic Review* 63: 50–72.

Rees, Albert, 1962.
The Economics of Trade Unions. Chicago: University of Chicago Press.

Rhodes, E. C., 1944.
"The Pareto Distribution of Incomes," *Econometrica* 12: 1–11.

Roy, A. D., 1950a.
"The Distribution of Earnings and of Individual Output," *Economic Journal* 60: 489–505.

———, 1950b.
"A Further Statistical Note on the Distribution of Individual Output," *Economic Journal* 60: 831–836.

———, 1951.
"Some Thoughts on the Distribution of Earnings," *Oxford Economic Papers* 3: 135–146.

Rutherford, R. S. G., 1955.
"Income Distribution: A New Model," *Econometrica* 23: 277–294.

Samuelson, Paul A., 1956.
"Social Indifference Curves," *Quarterly Journal of Economics* 70: 1–22.

———, 1969.
"Lifetime Portfolio Selection by Dynamic Stochastic Programming," *Review of Economics and Statistics* 51: 239–246.

Sargan, J. D., 1957.
"The Distribution of Wealth," *Econometrica* 25: 568–590.

Sato, Kazuo, 1971.
"Inheritance Taxation and the Personal Saving Incentive," SUNY at Buffalo Discussion Paper No. 180.

Shoup, Carl S., 1966.
Federal Estate and Gift Taxes. Washington: The Brookings Institution.

Solow, Robert M., 1951.
On the Dynamics of the Income Distribution, Unpublished Ph.D. dissertation. Harvard University.

————, 1960.
"Income Inequality Since the War," in R. E. Freeman (ed.), *Postwar Economic Trends in the United States.* New York: Harper and Row.

Soltow, Lee, 1965.
Towards Income Equality in Norway. Madison, Wis.; University of Wisconsin Press.

Somers, Harold M., 1965.
Capital Gains, Death and Gift Taxation. Sacramento: California Legislature.

Staehle, Hans, 1943.
"Ability, Wages and Income," *Review of Economics and Statistics* 25: 77–87.

Stiglitz, Joseph E., 1969.
"Distribution of Income and Wealth Among Individuals," *Econometrica* 37: 382–397.

Strotz, Robert H., 1955–1956.
"Myopia and Inconsistency in Dynamic Utility Maximization," *Review of Economic Studies* 23: 165–180.

Summers, Robert, 1956.
"An Econometric Investigation of the Size Distribution of Lifetime Average Annual Income," *Technical Report No. 31,* Stanford University.

Survey Research Center, 1970.
A Panel Study of Income Dynamics: Study Design, Procedures, Available Data, 1968–1970 Interviewing Years (Waves I-III). Ann Arbor: Survey Research Center.

Taubman, Paul J. and Terence J. Wales, 1973.
"Higher Education, Mental Ability, and Screening," *Journal of Political Economy* 81: 28–55.

Tawney, Richard H., 1952.
Equality, Fourth Edition. London: George Allen and Unwin.

Tinbergen, Jan, 1951.
"Some Remarks on the Distribution of Labour Incomes," *International Economic Papers* 1: 195–207.

————, 1956.
"On the Theory of Income Distribution," *Weltwirtschaftliches Archiv* 81: 155–175. Reprinted in his *Selected Papers* (Amsterdam: 1959), pp. 243–263.

————, 1957.
"Welfare Economics and Income Distribution," *American Economic Review, Papers and Proceedings* 47: 490–503.

————, 1971.
"A Positive and a Normative Theory of Income Distribution," *Review of Income and Wealth* 16: 221–234.

U.S. Bureau of the Census, 1970.
Statistical Abstract of the United States, 1970. Washington; U.S. Government Printing Office.

U.S. Internal Revenue Service, 1970.
Statistics of Income - 1968: Individual Income Tax Returns. Washington: U.S. Government Printing Office.

———, 1972.
Statistics of Income - 1969: Estate Tax Returns. Washington: U.S. Government Printing Office.

U.S. President, 1971.
Economic Report of the President, 1971. Washington: U.S. Government Printing Office.

Uzawa, Hirofumi, 1968a.
"Time Preference, The Consumption Function, and Optimum Asset Holdings," in J. N. Wolfe (ed.), *Value, Capital and Growth: Papers in Honour of Sir John Hicks.* Edinburgh: Edinburgh University Press.

———, 1968b.
"Market Allocation and Optimum Growth," *Australian Economic Papers* 7: 17–27.

Waldorf, William H., 1967.
"The Responsiveness of Federal Personal Income Taxes to Income Change," *Survey of Current Business* 47(April): 32–45.

Wallich, Henry C., 1960.
The Cost of Freedom. New York: Harper and Row.

Weizsäcker, Christian C. von, 1967.
"Training Policies under Conditions of Technical Progress: A Theoretical Treatment," in *Mathematical Models in Educational Planning.* Paris: O.E.C.D.

———, 1971.
"Notes on Endogenous Change of Tastes," *Journal of Economic Theory* 3: 345–372.

Wold, H. O. A., and P. Whittle, 1957.
"A Model Explaining the Pareto Distribution of Wealth," *Econometrica* 25: 591–595.

Yaari, Menahem E., 1964.
"On the Consumer's Lifetime Allocation Process," *International Economic Review* 5: 304–317.

———, 1965.
"Uncertain Lifetime, Life Insurance, and the Theory of the Consumer," *Review of Economic Studies* 32: 137–150.

Index